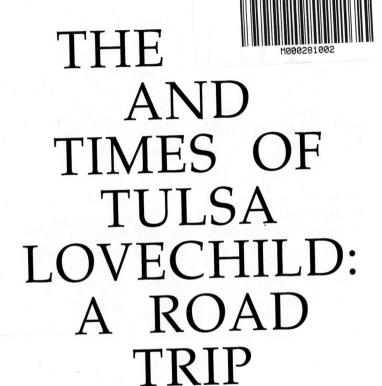

THE
AND
TIMES OF
TULSA
LOVECHILD:
A ROAD
TRIP

Greg Owens

BROADWAY PLAY PUBLISHING INC
56 E 81st St., NY NY 10028-0202
212 772-8334 fax: 212 772-8358
http://www.BroadwayPlayPubl.com

THE LIFE AND TIMES OF TULSA LOVECHILD:
A ROAD TRIP
© Copyright 2004 by Greg Owens

First printing: May 2004
I S B N: 0-88145-239-4

Book design: Marie Donovan
Word processing: Microsoft Word for Windows
Typographic controls: Xerox Ventura Publisher 2.0 P E
Typeface: Palatino
Printed on recycled acid-free paper and bound in the
U S A

ABOUT THE AUTHOR

Greg Owens was born and raised in southern Indiana, and received his M F A in Playwriting from Indiana University in 1993. He has written more than forty full-length plays, one-acts, and monologues that have been produced around the country.

As a writer for the Chicago-based interactive media company Jellyvision, Greg worked on the popular C D-ROM trivia games *You Don't Know Jack* and *Who Wants to Be a Millionaire?* He has also written for the C B C television show *Shift T V* in Toronto.

The Collaboraction Theater Company production of THE LIFE AND TIMES OF TULSA LOVECHILD was named the Best Off-Loop Play of 2001 by the Chicago Tribune and was nominated for seven Jefferson Awards. In 2003, Greg directed the play's Southeast premiere at the Warehouse Theater in Greenville, SC.

Greg lives in Bozeman, Montana with his wife Lila Michael and his daughter Lorelei Pearl.

THE LIFE AND TIMES OF TULSA LOVECHILD was first produced on 10 April 1998 by the Subterranean Theater Company (Tom Sonnek, Producer) at the Eclectic Theater in North Hollywood, California. The cast and creative contributors were:

BOB .... Tom Sonnek
WOODY .... Matt Caton
SYLVIA .... Cindy Sherbrooke
TULSA ....Chrissy Sonnek
STOCKTON, AGENT #1, & MEDIC #1 .... Steve Lee
ED ....Jeremy Hall
BABE/MAGGIE ....Tania Gutsche
STANLEY & AGENT #2 .... Stephen J Skelton
ROSE .... Lora Caton
VALERIE .... Molly Sullivan
MISS NEBRASKA .... Sarah Anderson
CLYDE & MEDIC #2 .... Ryan Sickler
MELVIN .... David Waterman

Director ....C Russell Muth
Set ....Michael J Riha
Lights ....Keith Morrison
Sound .... Greg Owens
Costumes .... Barbara Sculati
Music ....Matthew Ramsay
Stage manager .... Al Hayes

CHARACTERS & SETTING

BOB, *Russian dissident; motel owner*
WOODY, TULSA's *father; Vietnam-era activist; later a soldier*
SYLVIA, TULSA's *mother; former activist*
TULSA, *a graduate student*
STOCKTON, *retired C I A operative,* TULSA's *stepfather*
ED CARIBOU, *a former child actor; star of T V's* Johnny
Buckskin, Boy Detective
BABE*, ED's *co-star*
STANLEY, *director of* Johnny Buckskin; ED's *friend*
ROSE & VALERIE, *adult conjoined twins; friends of* BOB
MISS NEBRASKA, *a beauty queen*
MAGGIE*, *a rental car clerk*
CLYDE, MISS NEBRASKA's *jealous boyfriend*
MELVIN, *Army sergeant; later a U S Senator; then the leader
  of the quasi-militant Church of the Howling Savior, who
gets
  killed and comes back from beyond as a real-estate developer*
AGENT #1** & AGENT #2**, *Government agents*
MEDIC #1** & MEDIC #2**, *Vietnam-era Army medics*

*can be doubled by same actress
**can be doubled by STOCKTON/CLYDE/STANLEY)

*Time: 2002; August 1968; points in between and outside of
time.*

Place: The Road

This play is dedicated to Lila, Dennis, Russell, and Tom;
who believed in it from the beginning.

"We are not satisfied with faith...we demand to
experience the evidence."
—R D Laing, *The Politics of Experience*

"Don't let the past remind us of what we are not now."
—Crosby, Stills & Nash

ACT ONE: BORN TO RUN

PROLOGUE
THE ELVIS PRESLEY OF CIVIL ENGINEERING

(Lights up on the office of Bob's Exit 238 American Motel, a timeless oasis of American roadside kitsch and comfort. There's a counter, a clock, a calendar, and a few travel brochures. BOB is discovered in the office with a suitcase. He sets it down and addresses the audience.)

BOB: Hello. My name is Yuri Pavlovich Andropov. Call me Bob. This is where I live. I have been the owner-operator of "Bob's Exit 238 American Motel" here in Tulsa, Oklahoma since defecting from the former Soviet Union in 1966 under circumstances which I do not discuss. *(Beat)* You will say it is most strange that a Russian dissident should escape from behind the Iron Curtain and end up running a roadside motel in the American Southwest in the late 1960s. And I will tell you that you are right. Nonetheless, here I am. *(Beat)* And if accepting this is difficult for you, I assure you that you will soon be *convinced* I am a big, fat liar when I tell you about some of the people whose journeys have brought them here to Bob's.

(As BOB is speaking to the audience, WOODY and SYLVIA enter the motel office. They are dressed circa 1968 in "hippie" clothes. SYLVIA is pregnant. WOODY carries their bags. They look around the place and find no one there. They wait.)

BOB: But what can I say? Fact is stranger than fiction, and both of them are small potatoes compared to the stories I will tell you. But first, the prologue...

(Lights change. BOB *crosses D S C.)*

BOB: The greatest accomplishment of human beings in the history of the world is the American Interstate Highway System. Bigger than aqueducts of Rome. Egyptian pyramids? No way. The Interstate Highway System is the Elvis Presley—

*(*WOODY *rings the bell on the counter.* BOB *hesitates, then continues.)*

BOB: It is the Elvis Presley of Civil Engineering.
I get in my car. Portland, Maine. I drive one week, maybe less. I am in San Francisco, California.
Three thousand, one-hundred and seventy-five miles.
It's nothing. (Snaps fingers) Like that.

*(*WOODY *rings the bell.)*

BOB: And everywhere there's gas for the car, food for the people. Motels. Phone booths. Scenic overlooks. Points of historical interest and natural phenomena beyond belief. *(Beat)* A man came here and told me he saw the World's Largest Hand-Dug Well in Kansas. Literally knocked my socks off.

*(*WOODY *rings the bell.* BOB *looks anxiously toward him, but continues.)*

BOB: Stonehenge? What's that? A pile of rocks.

*(*WOODY *rings the bell.)*

BOB: Interstate Highway Systems is...

*(*WOODY *rings the bell.* BOB *turns to him.)*

BOB: I am coming in one minute.

*(*BOB *looks at the audience, tries to regroup.* WOODY *rings the bell. That does it.)*

BOB: The prologue is over.

(Lights fade.)

(Up-tempo music with a sixties feel plays, accompanied by a video projection. The projection should be something simple; perhaps rapidly flashing images of the center yellow lines on the highway. Superimposed above the image, the title "The Life and Times of Tulsa Lovechild" flashes onto the screen. Next, the words "a road trip" appear, then both titles flash away.)

(Note: All scene and act titles should also be projected.)

(Fade to black. Music out.)

I.01
UTOPIAN DISSONANCE; OR THE POLITICS OF UNDEREMPLOYMENT

(In one area of the stage, TULSA sits. She wears what for her are job interview clothes, and a beaded necklace. It is 2002.)

(On the other side of the stage, WOODY and SYLVIA walk into their motel room. SYLVIA falls into the bed. It is 1968—for now.)

TULSA: *(To interviewer)* Hello. I'm Tulsa. Tulsa Lovechild. *(She manufactures an awkward smile.)* Yes, I've been told it's an unusual name. It also spells "A slut" backwards, as I learned in junior high. *(Beat)* My parents... *(TULSA ironically flashes a peace sign.)* It's a 60s thing. *(Beat)* Well, to make a long story short: I was born in a motel room in Tulsa, Oklahoma during the "summer of love." *(Beat)* All things considered, I feel fortunate not to have wound up "Rainbow" or "Freedom."

(Scene shifts to WOODY and SYLVIA while lights remain up on TULSA.)

WOODY: Freedom?

SYLVIA: Yeah.

WOODY: You can't be serious.

SYLVIA: You don't like it?

WOODY: No.

TULSA: Yeah. Good thing my mother wasn't Grace Slick. You could be interviewing *god* right now.

SYLVIA: What's wrong with Freedom?

WOODY: I'd rather not do that to a kid.

SYLVIA: Do what? I think it's a beautiful name.

WOODY: Somehow I don't think the 3rd grade bully's going to agree with you.

TULSA: *(Explaining her joke)* You know, Grace Slick? *(Beat)* How old are you? Sorry. Never mind. *(Beat)* Anyway, I got my undergraduate degree in psychology from Montana State University— *(Listens)* Well, I sort of grew up in a lot of places actually. Wherever the van broke down. We moved to Bozeman with my stepfather Stockton when he retired from the CIA, so that's how I ended up in Montana. *(Listens, with a grimace, forces a laugh)* Unabomber. That's a good one. *(Changing subject)* So, next I got an M.A. in American Studies from UM in Missoula and I'm currently at the University of Washington here in Seattle. *(Listens, answers)* I'm working on a doctoral thesis called "Ironic Fatalism in the Music of Bob Dylan" for a Ph.D in Comp Lit. *(Explaining)* Comparative Literature. *(With thinly concealed contempt)* Yeah. Sorta like English.

SYLVIA: So, what you're saying is you want to teach our child to acquiesce to societal pressure before she's even born?

WOODY: I'm sorry. Could you spell that for me?

SYLVIA: You know what I mean.

WOODY: Maybe if you could say it in English.

SYLVIA: Look Woody, just because you're back in Oklahoma don't put on the Tom Joad routine, all right? I don't buy it.

WOODY: I'm sorry. I didn't realize that I was still required to be intellectually hip once we left Berkeley.

SYLVIA: Stop putting it down. You go to school there too.

WOODY: *(Correcting her)* I used to.

SYLVIA: Well you still would if it weren't for those asshole Nazis in the Dean's office.

WOODY: *(Ironically)* Yeah, can you believe the nerve of those guys? Somebody steals all the files out of their office and burns them and they kick the guy outta school. For nothin'.

SYLVIA: I think it was a righteous thing you did. A lot of people thought so.

WOODY: I'm afraid I don't have my liberal thesaurus with me. Is "righteous" another word for "stupid"?

TULSA: Yes. I'm familiar with Microsoft Word, Excel, Lotus and PowerPoint. I've worked with several database programs and I can type about seventy-five words per minute. Eighty with coffee.

WOODY: What are we even doing here? It's thirty more miles to my parents' house.

SYLVIA: I'm not in the mood for the Lawrence Welk show and the pledge of allegiance tonight, okay?

WOODY: Well, you better get used to it.

SYLVIA: What's that supposed to mean?

WOODY: You're gonna be staying there while I'm gone.

SYLVIA: Oh no. *Hell* no!

WOODY: I made arrangements with my folks—

SYLVIA: Hold on. Who the fuck do you think you are making arrangements for me?

WOODY: I'm the father of that kid, that's who I am. And watch your mouth.

SYLVIA: Fuck you. You've got no right to make decisions for me.

WOODY: I just want what's best for you and the baby.

SYLVIA: If that were true you wouldn't be going anywhere.

WOODY: Don't start that again.

SYLVIA: I'm not staying with your parents, Woody.

WOODY: All right then. What's your plan?

SYLVIA: I'm going to Chicago.

WOODY: What are you gonna do, Sylvia? March in the streets with a newborn baby?

SYLVIA: You bet your ass I am. And you should be there too.

WOODY: You know I can't do that.

SYLVIA: *(Indicating the baby)* Then we're going alone.

TULSA: *(Indicating her necklace)* This? Oh, my mom makes them. *(Somewhat defensively)* Yes. I suppose it is "interesting."

WOODY: What difference does it make? Do you really think you're gonna stop the war?

SYLVIA: Yes I do. I believe that this is our moment in history to do something miraculous.

WOODY: Yeah well, I wish it were our moment in history to have some gas money.

SYLVIA: I'm sorry that the novelty has worn off for you, Woody. But this isn't a game to me. I care about what's going on over there and I'm not going to just sit around and bake cookies while these fat old liars drink the blood of another generation. I think our child deserves a better world than that.

WOODY: What do you want me to do? I pissed away my student deferment. I can either report to the draft board or I can go to jail.

TULSA: What exactly do you mean when you say "team player"?

SYLVIA: We could go to Canada.

WOODY: I can't run.

TULSA: My greatest weakness? Excuse me?

SYLVIA: Please don't go.

TULSA: Look, Junior. I'm thirty-four years old, all right? I started college when you were still running around in your Incredible Hulk Underoos. I'm hopelessly over-educated and I've never had a job that paid more than the monthly salary of a Chilean garbage man. And all I'm trying to do here is make a little money so I can register for some more absolutely useless classes so I can hopefully delay for a few more months the beginning of what will be the rest of my life's work of paying off school loans. And please correct me if I'm wrong, but I have a damn good hunch that regardless of my answers to your idiotic questions, and even if my greatest weakness were an uncontrollable glue-sniffing habit, I think that I could still probably manage to answer your goddamn phone. Don't ya think? So all I really need to hear from you is can I have this stupid job or not? *(Beat)* Thank you. Of course. I understand.

(TULSA *stands and starts to walk away. She stops and watches as* WOODY *kisses* SYLVIA *and then walks slowly away from her, offstage.*)

TULSA: Mom?

SYLVIA: Yes dear?

TULSA: Why didn't you insist that I become a lawyer?

SYLVIA: Did you want to be a lawyer?

TULSA: Of course not.

SYLVIA: But I should have made you.

TULSA: Not necessarily. But I think that perhaps somewhere in between "Blowing in the Wind" and Composting 1-0-1 we might have had a little talk about economic survival.

SYLVIA: Well I'm sorry I didn't raise you to be a better receptionist, Tulsa.

(*A cordless phone rings on-stage.* TULSA *answers it.*)

TULSA: Hello?

(*Lights discover* STOCKTON *in another area of the stage. He's dressed in insulated overalls with a hunter's orange jacket and cap.*)

STOCKTON: Did I ever tell you about the mess they got me into in sixty-five? Oakland?

TULSA: (*Holds hand over phone, to* SYLVIA) Great. It's your husband.

STOCKTON: Some genius in Domestic Operations cooked the whole thing up. Get the Angels to get Castro. Right. See that marching down Main Street in your mother's girdle. Bend over, Stockton. This is a job for you.

TULSA: (*To* SYLVIA) Tell me again how this man became my stepfather?

STOCKTON: Get your teeth knocked out with a Harley chain by some three hundred-pound brute's got a head full of Owsley's Brain Drano and fewer chromosomes than a fucking sea monkey—

TULSA: Whoa! Stockton! Cold war's over. Your side won.

STOCKTON: Hello girl.

TULSA: Stockton, what's wrong?

STOCKTON: Your mother.

TULSA: What is it? *(Beat)* She's dead, isn't she?

STOCKTON: Affirmative.

(TULSA *drops her hand to her side, still holding the phone. She looks at* SYLVIA.)

STOCKTON: She's gone, girl.

(*Lights fade on* STOCKTON.)

TULSA: Mom...

SYLVIA: I guess that doctor was being overly optimistic when he said I had a year.

TULSA: Oh God.

SYLVIA: Now listen, I've left instructions with Stockton to take part of my ashes and scatter them up at Mystic Lake. I was going to have him mail the rest to you but I don't trust the postal service, so you'll have to come to Montana to get them because I've got another place in mind for you.

TULSA: Where?

(*Lights come up on* BOB *in the office. As* SYLVIA *answers the question,* BOB *looks at the audience as if to say "you guessed it!"*)

SYLVIA: Bob's Exit 238 American Motel in beautiful Tulsa, Oklahoma.

(Lights out on BOB.*)*

TULSA: What?

SYLVIA: It's right outside of town on I-44.

TULSA: You're kidding.

SYLVIA: Tulsa, why would I be kidding?

TULSA: Why there?

SYLVIA: Because that's what I want. For Pete's sake, Tulsa, I would think that this is one thing I could get you to do for me without an argument.

TULSA: I'm sorry. I didn't realize maternal guilt still worked in the afterlife.

SYLVIA: Some things are eternal, dear. Besides, you spend too much time inside anyway. I think a road trip would be good for you.

TULSA: Okay.

SYLVIA: Good.

TULSA: I love you, Mom.

SYLVIA: I love you too, honey. Now, if you hurry you can beat traffic.

(Lights fade.)

I.02
DAY OF RECKONING FOR THE BOY DETECTIVE

(Lights up on BOB *in the office.)*

BOB: *(To audience)* Danger. Excitement. Mystery. Romance. Violence. Sex. And emergency medical procedures...on this week's *Johnny Buckskin, Boy Detective.*

(Lights fade on BOB. ED *is discovered with* BABE. BABE *is a babe, clad in a bikini.* ED *wears no clothes that we can see. He holds a giant beach ball in front of him.)*

ED: But wait! There's more! What were you doing last night at 10 o'clock?

BABE: I was with you. Remember?

ED: That's right. Well then, in that case, what are you doing tonight?

BABE: Going back to your place for more questioning?

ED: *(Seductively)* And some fingerprinting?

BABE: Don't you want to put some clothes on?

ED: *(Patting beach ball)* I think I've got it covered.

STANLEY: *(O S)* CUT!

ED: *(Angrily)* What?

*(*STANLEY *storms on-stage.)*

STANLEY: Ed, could you just make believe you know how to act long enough for me to wrap this fucking scene? Huh? I don't ask much, all right? Fake it, okay? Same thing I told all three of my wives. Just give me the impression you give half a shit once in a while, I'm happy.

(While STANLEY *is talking,* ED *drops the beach ball. He is wearing a pair of Speedos. He reaches inside them and takes out a pack of cigarettes and a lighter. He smokes.)*

ED: Have you had somebody read this script to you, Stanley? This thing sucks worse than Ms. Hoover over there.

BABE: Hey!

ED & STANLEY: Shut up!

(BABE *takes the beach ball and exits in a huff.*)

STANLEY: Listen, Ed. If you have a problem with the script you can tell me.

ED: I have a problem with the script, Stanley.

STANLEY: Well who the fuck are you, F Scott Fitzsimmons all the sudden? You're an actor. Do your job. Shut your mouth and say your lines!

ED: I can't do this anymore, Stan. I can't stand in a pile of shit and pretend I don't smell it.

STANLEY: Look, Ed, don't start with this "I wanna do theater" crap on me again, okay? Do I have to remind you? What was it? Two performances of Hamlet. They could hear Shakespeare puking in his grave all the way from La Jolla.

ED: Nothing feels right anymore, Stanley.

STANLEY: Have you gotten laid recently?

ED: I need to do something worthwhile—

STANLEY: Like I said—

ED: —with my life.

STANLEY: Like what, Ed? What are you going to do? Tell me what normal and decent thing you can actually imagine yourself doing?

ED: Maybe I need to figure that out.

STANLEY: Yeah, well maybe I need to stop drinking martinis for breakfast, too, but certain things are in our Nature, Ed. *(Beat)* Look, Eddie, I understand how you're feeling. Believe me, I do. There's always doubt. Uncertainty. Is what we do worth doing? Does it really mean shit to anybody? I'm fairly certain that it doesn't, Ed. We do this show. Certain people watch it. Certain others use it to sell tampons and minivans. These other guys over here, they give us a rather large pile of money to produce the thing that sells the tampons that makes everybody else money. Then we do it again. It's all habit, Ed. It's not entirely bad. It's not entirely good. It's what we do.

ED: Does that satisfy you, Stanley?

STANLEY: Who's satisfied? All I know is I got the daughters of Lucifer eating my balls for lunch if I don't pay alimony. It keeps me focused. (*Trying to comfort him*) Ed, your life could suck much worse.

ED: Thanks, Stanley. I appreciate that.

STANLEY: Hey. I appreciate you, Edwardo.

ED: I quit, Stan.

STANLEY: You what?

ED: I quit. (*He exits.*)

STANLEY: I hope your guts boil in Hell, you rotten bastard!

(*Blackout*)

I.03
ROSE & VALERIE PLOT THEIR ESCAPE FROM THE CHURCH OF THE HOWLING SAVIOR

(*Lights discover* BOB.)

BOB: (*To audience*) Meanwhile, at the Church of the Howling Savior compound in Kansas... Rose and Valerie plot their escape.

(*Lights FADE on* BOB *as we discover* ROSE *and* VALERIE. *On the floor in front of them are two enormous dog food bowls.* ROSE *and* VALERIE *struggle to open a ten-pound bag of dog food. This task is complicated by the fact that they are conjoined twins, joined at the hip.)*

(Throughout the scene, the periodic yelping and barking of coyotes is heard off-stage.)

ROSE: Hold that end, Valerie.

VALERIE: I'm trying.

(As they succeed in opening the bag, dog food spills everywhere. ROSE and VALERIE fall over. The barking gets momentarily louder.)

ROSE: Great. Didn't I tell you to hold on?

VALERIE: I tried, Rose. I couldn't hold it. You're stronger than I am.

ROSE: Well, don't just sit there making excuses. Help me get up.

VALERIE: Ready? One, two, three...

(With a coordinated, but rather awkward effort, ROSE and VALERIE manage to lift themselves up off the floor.)

ROSE: Oh, for Christ's sake, would you look at this mess?

VALERIE: Rose!

ROSE: Don't start with me, Valerie.

VALERIE: Please don't take the Lord's name in vain.

ROSE: If you don't like it, leave the room.

VALERIE: That isn't funny, Rose.

ROSE: Help me clean this up. We've got to get ready.

(ROSE and VALERIE scoop up the dog food and put it in the bowls.)

VALERIE: I still don't know if I feel right about this.

ROSE: Valerie, we've been over this. We've got to stick to the plan.

VALERIE: But Father Melvin has been so good to us. I don't know if I want to leave The Family.

ROSE: Father Melvin is a fraud, Valerie. He's getting rich off this whole scam. How can you still refuse to see that?

VALERIE: I don't like to hear you refer to the church as a "scam."

ROSE: Scam, racket, con—whatever you wanna call it. He's been raking it in from all of us for years. And I don't know about you, but I've had it.

VALERIE: Oh, Rose, I just hate to believe it. I've liked living here at the compound. The Family has been like, well, like a family to us.

ROSE: The Family are even bigger kooks than our own family, Valerie.

VALERIE: Rose, that isn't nice.

(ROSE *smacks* VALERIE's *head.*)

ROSE: Hello! Any brains on that side? These people are wackos!

VALERIE: The Family has been very kind to us, Rose. They've been much nicer than the people at the carnival. You have to admit that.

ROSE: All I know is I want out of here before they start passing around the Kool-Aid and apple sauce.

VALERIE: Your heart is so full of hate.

ROSE: Yeah well, I'm a lousy dancer too, but we live with our faults.

(*Beat*)

VALERIE: I'll leave if you want to.

ROSE: Good. So that's settled.

VALERIE: But I won't help you steal from Father Melvin.

ROSE: We're not stealing from him, Valerie. We're taking back our own money.

VALERIE: We never gave him as much as you're talking about. We couldn't have.

ROSE: So call it interest.

VALERIE: It's not right, Rose.

ROSE: Right? What do you call right, Valerie? Living like this our whole lives? Is that right?

VALERIE: We're fortunate to have lived at all, Rose.

ROSE: That's not enough. Not anymore.

(Beat)

VALERIE: You really think it'll work?

ROSE: All we have to do is sneak away to his office during the evening service.

VALERIE: No. Not that. I mean the other thing.

ROSE: The operation?

VALERIE: Yes.

ROSE: Well, look at it this way, sis. What have we got to lose?

VALERIE: Just each other.

ROSE: Amen to that. Come on. Let's feed these mutts and get out of here.

(ROSE and VALERIE carry the dog food bowls off-stage. The coyotes howl with anticipation. Blackout)

I.04
MOURNING RUSH

(TULSA *stands at an airport rental counter with the clerk,*
MAGGIE. SYLVIA *stands nearby.*)

MAGGIE: Name?

TULSA: Tulsa Lovechild.

MAGGIE: *(Typing)* Tulsa...

TULSA: Lovechild. *(Makes peace sign)* My parents were
hippies.

MAGGIE: Mm-hm.

SYLVIA: *(To TULSA)* I hate that word.

TULSA: Would you prefer "flower children"?

SYLVIA: It just reduces all those lives, all that experience,
to a label.

TULSA: Sorry, mother. Everybody gets a box; in you go.
(Watching MAGGIE type) Lovechild. One word.

MAGGIE: Oh.

TULSA: Good thing my mother wasn't Grace Slick.

MAGGIE: *(Engrossed in the screen)* Yes.

TULSA: You'd be renting a car to *god* right now.

MAGGIE: *(Looking up)* I'm sorry?

TULSA: Never mind.

MAGGIE: Okay.

SYLVIA: Tulsa, no one under fifty is ever going to get
that joke.

MAGGIE: Destination?

TULSA: Oklahoma.

MAGGIE: O K.

TULSA: Tulsa.

MAGGIE: *(Stops typing)* So...your name is Tulsa and you're going to Tulsa.

TULSA: *(A hint of condescension)* How about that?

SYLVIA: Be nice.

TULSA: *(Smiling, to MAGGIE)* Yes.

MAGGIE: Okay.

TULSA: *(To SYLVIA)* Why?

SYLVIA: Why what?

TULSA: After all this time. Why do you want me to take you back there?

SYLVIA: I don't know if I could explain it in a way that would make sense to you.

TULSA: Give it a shot.

SYLVIA: Do you really have to have a reason?

TULSA: I think it would help, yes.

SYLVIA: Sometimes experience is its own justification, Tulsa.

TULSA: Yes mother, thank you, and I don't need a weatherman to know which way the wind blows, I know. It's all very lovely, but could you please tell me why I'm driving half-way across the country to dump your ashes at a truck stop?

SYLVIA: It's not a truck stop—

TULSA: Whatever.

MAGGIE: Credit card?

TULSA: *(To MAGGIE)* I'm sorry?

MAGGIE: What credit card will that be on?

(TULSA *hands her a credit card.*)

MAGGIE: Thank you.

SYLVIA: I think you'll find an energy there that will be good for you.

(*Incredulous,* TULSA *snaps her fingers, beatnik style, at* SYLVIA.)

TULSA: Oh wow. Thanks, man.

SYLVIA: That was a beatnik thing, dear. *Hippies* didn't do that.

TULSA: You know, Paradise Valley I could understand. Berkeley? Sure. Even the place in New Mexico, the commune—

SYLVIA: (*Remembering it more fondly*) The Peace Farm.

TULSA: With the goats? Ugh.

MAGGIE: (*To* TULSA) Would you like insurance with that?

TULSA: Excuse me?

MAGGIE: Insurance?

TULSA: Yes. And some fries.

(MAGGIE *stares blankly at* TULSA.)

TULSA: Never mind. It was a joke.

MAGGIE: Oh.

TULSA: He left you there alone, Mom.

SYLVIA: I wasn't alone. I had you.

TULSA: Please. (*She momentarily decides to forget the whole thing. To* MAGGIE) You know what? I'm sorry. Was it Patty?

MAGGIE: (*Indicating her name badge*) Maggie.

TULSA: Maggie.

MAGGIE: Yes.

TULSA: I'm sorry.

MAGGIE: Oh no—

TULSA: Maggie—

MAGGIE: Yes?

TULSA: Here's the thing—

MAGGIE: Uh-huh?

(TULSA *looks at* SYLVIA, *decides to go ahead.*)

TULSA: *(To* MAGGIE*)* Can I get unlimited mileage with that?

MAGGIE: Oh you bet.

TULSA: *(To* SYLVIA*)* This is really crazy. You know that, don't you? I mean, even for you this is eccentric.

SYLVIA: Drive safely, dear.

MAGGIE: *(Handing keys to* TULSA*)* Drive safely!

(Blackout)

I.05
A BRUTISH DISPLAY OF MISGUIDED MACHISMO COSTS MISS NEBRASKA VITAL POINTS IN THE TALENT COMPETITION

(Lights cross fade to another area of the stage where MISS NEBRASKA *stands in front of a microphone. She is dressed in high heels and a bathing suit, with the obligatory state identification banner.)*

MISS NEBRASKA: Good evening ladies and gentlemen. My name is Kelli Jo Daugherty, Miss— *(Turns, offstage)* Are all these lights gonna be here when we do it for

real? I can't see a thing. I feel like a treed coon. *(Gasps)*
Oh, Miss Alabama, I'm so sorry. I meant a raccoon,
I swear. *(Beat)* What? Oh. Okay. I'm sorry. *(Takes a
moment to remember her place)* Oh ... um, Kelli Jo
Daugherty, Miss Nebraska. And I believe that all of
us under the sun are God's beloved children. Red
and yellow, black and white—just like the song says.
The strength of America is in her diversity. It's time we
celebrate the differences that make us great and tear
down the barriers that stand between us—

*(CLYDE rushes on-stage with a shotgun. MISS NEBRASKA
screams.)*

MISS NEBRASKA: Clyde! What are you doing here?

CLYDE: Get your clothes on, Kelli Jo. We're goin' home.

MISS NEBRASKA: I'm rehearsing, you moron!

CLYDE: I don't care what you're doin'. You're comin'
with me.

*(CLYDE hefts her up over his shoulder with one arm.
MISS NEBRASKA yells and screams in protest.)*

MISS NEBRASKA: Let me go, you stupid ape! Help! Help!
I'm bein' kidnapped!! Help!

*(Lights rise on BOB as CLYDE deposits MISS NEBRASKA in
the front seat of his combine and drives away.)*

BOB: Mad with jealousy, young Clyde had driven
day and night in his John Deere combine. All the way
from Kearney, Nebraska to Atlantic City to retrieve the
woman he loved. With each passing mile, as fields of
wheat gave way to green corn and the green turned
into the million neon colors of the East, noble Clyde
fancied himself a romantic hero. A Robin Hood—

CLYDE: Batman.

BOB: Yes—

CLYDE: Spiderman.

BOB: These and others, yes. And he was sure that his beloved damsel in distress would melt into his arms and weep with loving joy when at last he had rescued her.

MISS NEBRASKA: GODDAMN STUPID STUBBORN SELFISH PIG-HEADED PEA-BRAINED BUTT-SCRATCHIN' FINGER-SNIFFIN' IDIOTIC NO GOOD INBRED PINHEAD BAG OF BOILED SKUNK PISS!

BOB: This did not happen.

CLYDE: I love you, Kelli Jo.

MISS NEBRASKA: GO TO HELL!

CLYDE: I mean it. I love you!

MISS NEBRASKA: GO TO HELL!!

CLYDE: I LOVE YOU, KELLI JO!

MISS NEBRASKA: GO TO HELL!!!

(Blackout)

I.06
HALF HIPPIE TILL THE END

(Lights up on STOCKTON in his living room in Montana. He sits in a chair holding something in his lap which is not yet visible to the audience. There is an elk skin on the floor in front of him.)

(TULSA enters.)

TULSA: Hey, Stockton. (Looks at elk skin) Hello dead thing.

STOCKTON: John Lennon was a drug fiend and a communist queer. You know that, don't you?

TULSA: You've mentioned it before, yes.

STOCKTON: If you're here for money, I don't have any. I sent it all to some crank preacher in Kansas. Says he's got coyotes speaking in tongues. Howling the word of God, he says. Gonna train 'em to eat the non-believers alive. Breed 'em, set 'em loose by the hundreds in all the major cities. Crazy bastard's got a sense of poetry.

TULSA: I don't want money.

STOCKTON: Didn't bring any of your hippie friends with you?

TULSA: I'm not a hippie, Stockton. I've got too many credit cards.

STOCKTON: Got my elk.

TULSA: So I see.

(STOCKTON *holds up a funerary urn with a Deadhead sticker on it. He shows it to* TULSA.)

STOCKTON: That was her idea. She was about half hippie right up till the end. Never cured her off it.

TULSA: *(Smiles)* No, I guess not.

STOCKTON: They never forgave her for hooking up with me. They stood right outside the church the day we got hitched. With their signs. You remember that?

(TULSA *nods.*)

STOCKTON: Now you tell me what kind of freaks protest a wedding?

TULSA: I think it was a little hard for some of Mom's friends to understand. I mean, you were infiltrating them when you met her.

STOCKTON: Well, I guess it wasn't your typical boy-meets-girl scenario.

(*They both laugh.*)

TULSA: Not exactly.

STOCKTON: All kinds of people fall in love.

TULSA: You gonna be all right, Stockton?

STOCKTON: I'll give 'em a good fight before they get me.

TULSA: Okay.

(STOCKTON *hands her the urn. She starts to leave.*)

STOCKTON: Hey! Girl!

TULSA: *(Turning)* Tulsa.

STOCKTON: Right.

TULSA: You always just called me "girl."

STOCKTON: It's a—what do you call it?

TULSA: Noun.

STOCKTON: A term.

TULSA: Yes.

STOCKTON: Of endearment.

TULSA: It is?

STOCKTON: Not a good one. But what the hell. I'm not John Denver.

(TULSA *laughs.*)

STOCKTON: Don't use your turn signal.

TULSA: Why?

STOCKTON: That's how they track you. *(Explaining)* From the helicopters.

TULSA: All right. *(Beat)* Goodbye Stockton.

(STOCKTON *nods.* TULSA *exits.*)

(Blackout)

I.07
WAR! HUH! GOOD GOD!

(Lights come up on WOODY. *He is now dressed in combat fatigues and his head is shaved. He holds a weapon on his shoulder. Sergeant* MELVIN PIKE *stands in front of him and barks into his face.)*

MELVIN: ARE YOU WILLING TO GIVE YOU LIFE FOR YOUR COUNTRY?

*(*WOODY *hesitates.)*

MELVIN: DID YOU HEAR ME?

WOODY: I don't know, Sergeant Pike!

MELVIN: WHAT THE HELL KIND OF FAGGOT ANSWER IS THAT, YOU MISERABLE SACK OF DOGSHIT?

WOODY: Sergeant—

MELVIN: WILL YOU DIE DEFENDING THE UNITED STATES OF AMERICA?

WOODY: Yes Sergeant!

MELVIN: NO YOU WILL NOT, YOU IGNORANT SON-OF-A-BITCH!

WOODY: Sergeant—

MELVIN: "THE OBJECT OF WAR IS NOT TO DIE FOR YOUR COUNTRY BUT TO MAKE THE OTHER BASTARD DIE FOR HIS." DO YOU KNOW WHO SAID THAT, SOLDIER?

WOODY: George Patton, Sergeant!

MELVIN: GEORGE? ARE YOU THE MAN'S WIFE, SOLDIER?

WOODY: No Sergeant!

MELVIN: THEN THAT IS GENERAL GODDAMN PATTON TO YOU!

WOODY: YES SERGEANT PIKE!

(Blackout)

I.08
SOMEWHERE IN WYOMING

(Lights UP on TULSA, driving. Suddenly, ED runs out into the middle of the road in front of her. TULSA screams.)

(SFX: Brakes screeching)

(ED tumbles out of the way of the car and rolls to safety on the other side of the road.)

TULSA: Jesus Christ!

ED: I'm okay.

(TULSA gets out of the car. ED stands.)

TULSA: What in the hell do you think you're doing?

ED: I'm sorry. They were chasing me.

(TULSA looks around, sees no one.)

TULSA: Who?

(ED points to the side of the road.)

ED: Over there.

TULSA: I don't see anyone.

ED: Those things. There. They were chasing me.

TULSA: Those are antelope.

ED: *(Looks)* Antelope?

TULSA: They were chasing you?

ED: Yes.

(TULSA *laughs.*)

ED: It's not funny.

TULSA: Are you sure you're all right?

(ED *knocks the dust off.*)

ED: Yeah. I think so.

TULSA: You scared the hell out of me.

ED: I'm sorry.

TULSA: What are you doing out here?

ED: I've been trying to catch a ride. (*Looks up and down the road*) It's been pretty quiet though.

TULSA: No kidding. (*Takes a good look at him*) You're not from around here, are you?

ED: No, I'm from L A.

TULSA: Oh.

ED: What do you mean "oh"?

TULSA: Where did you break down?

ED: I didn't. (*Explaining*) I'm thumbing it.

TULSA: (*Incredulous*) What did you do, hitch-hike all the way here from California?

ED: Yes.

TULSA: Where are you headed?

ED: I don't know really.

TULSA: (*Crossing back to car*) Well, if I can give you a little advice, you ought to see if you can get yourself into Cheyenne and pick up a rental car. Nobody's going to pick you up in this country out here except people you don't want to have picking you up. And there's a few critters wandering around out here that are even scarier than antelope.

ED: Who are you, Grizzly Adams' daughter?

TULSA: I'm just somebody who grew up around here. What you're doing is foolish.

ED: How far is it to Cheyenne?

TULSA: A hundred miles.

ED: How am I supposed to get that far without taking a ride from someone?

TULSA: I don't know. But I'd try to do it quickly if I were you. (*She starts to get into her car.*)

ED: Wait! Couldn't you take me there?

TULSA: I don't pick up hitch-hikers.

ED: But you stopped.   -

TULSA: I stopped because I thought I'd killed you.

ED: Please—

TULSA: Listen, I wish I could help but I can't—

ED: I'm not dangerous. I swear.

TULSA: Well, of course not, because all of the dangerous people always announce it first thing.

ED: Do you know who I am?

TULSA: How would I know you?

(ED *gestures toward his face, certain that she will recognize him.*)

ED: Edward Caribou?

TULSA: You're asking me?

ED: No. That's my name.

TULSA: Well, good luck, Ed.

ED: No, wait! I'm an actor. (Laughs) Sorry. Never can say that with a straight face. I have a television show. *Johnny Buckskin, Boy Detective*?

(TULSA *shakes her head.*)

ED: You've never seen it?

TULSA: Sorry.

ED: You know ... (Assuming the role) "But wait! There's more!"

TULSA: I don't watch T V.

ED: Yeah, I know. Everybody says that. But, come on, you know me, right?

TULSA: Not from Adam.

ED: (Exasperated) No. Of course not.

TULSA: So long, Ed.

ED: Hey, come on, now. You can't leave me here. I'm scared. (Beat) I'll ride in the trunk if you want.

TULSA: What?

ED: If it would make you feel better, I'd be happy to ride in the trunk. Look, you know, I'm really not suited for this kind of thing. I know that now. I would never have even made it this far, except I caught one ride all the way here from Bakersfield. In the back of a cattle trailer! I mean, come on, Jesus Christ, I rode with cows for two days! You think I can't ride in your trunk for an hour! I'm begging you.

TULSA: Okay. Enough. Get in.

ED: Oh God, thank you. (He heads for the back of the car.)

TULSA: Get up here.

ED: What?

TULSA: You're not going to ride in my trunk.

ED: No, really, I'm happy to.

TULSA: Ed!

ED: Okay, okay. Front seat it is.

(ED *gets into the car.* TULSA *drives.*)

ED: I want you to know how much I appreciate this.

TULSA: You're welcome.

(*Beat*)

ED: You mind if I smoke?

TULSA: I'd rather you didn't.

ED: Of course.

TULSA: I can let you out.

ED: No, it's okay. I'll try breathing. (*Beat*) So...what's your name?

TULSA: Tulsa Lovechild.

ED: What are you, a country singer?

TULSA: Ed?

ED: Yes?

TULSA: Talking—

ED: Uh huh—

TULSA: —is not mandatory.

(*Blackout*)

I.09
STAND DOWN YOUR MAN

(CLYDE *stands with his back to the audience, taking a leak.* MISS NEBRASKA *enters with the shotgun. She points it at* CLYDE.)

MISS NEBRASKA: Listen up, Clyde.

CLYDE: Kelli Jo, what in the hell—

MISS NEBRASKA: Save it, Mister! I ought to blow your damn head off right now.

CLYDE: Now, honey, you don't wanna do that.

MISS NEBRASKA: I want to, Clyde. Believe me, I want to.

CLYDE: Can't we talk about this, honey?

MISS NEBRASKA: I'm done talkin' to you.

CLYDE: I just wanted you back home with me, darlin'.

MISS NEBRASKA: What about what I wanted, Clyde? You had any goddamn sense about you, you'd understand that some things in life are more important than whether you have to get up off your fat ass and get your own beer.

CLYDE: There's more to it than that, Kelli Jo. I love you.

MISS NEBRASKA: I'm talkin' now, Clyde! Shut your trap. Now get down on your knees.

(CLYDE *hesitates*.)

MISS NEBRASKA: Now!

CLYDE: Honey, I just took a whiz right here.

MISS NEBRASKA: Well, if you don't want that to be your last one ever, I suggest you get down like I tell you.

(CLYDE *kneels*.)

MISS NEBRASKA: I'm leavin', Clyde. And don't you even think about comin' after me again.

CLYDE: Kelli Jo—

MISS NEBRASKA: You know the Miss America song, Clyde?

CLYDE: The what?

MISS NEBRASKA: Miss America! The song!

CLYDE: Yeah. I think.

MISS NEBRASKA: When I count to three, I'm gonna start walkin' away and I wanna hear you singin'.

CLYDE: Kelli Jo, this is crazy, honey.

MISS NEBRASKA: One. *(She starts to back away.)*

CLYDE: Don't leave me.

MISS NEBRASKA: Two.

CLYDE: Honey?

MISS NEBRASKA: Three. *(Beat)* Three, Clyde!

CLYDE: *(Sings)* "There she is—"

MISS NEBRASKA: *Goes*, Clyde. There she goes.

CLYDE: *(Sings)* "There she goes, Miss America..."

(MISS NEBRASKA exits.)

CLYDE: "There she goes..." Honey! What's the rest of the words?

(Blackout)

I.10
LAMENT OF THE BOY DETECTIVE

(Lights discover TULSA and ED, driving.)

TULSA: So, you're the boy detective.

ED: Well, the show's been on for twelve years.

TULSA: Oh.

ED: You never saw it?

TULSA: No.

ED: Never?

TULSA: Sorry.

ED: Oh, no need to be sorry. *(Beat)* I just can't believe you haven't even heard of it.

TULSA: Nope.

ED: So, anyway, how do you like your job at the Arctic weather station? Those long months away from civilization must get tough, huh? No phone. Radio. T V.

TULSA: *(Laughs)* You're closer to the truth than you think. I'm a graduate student at the University of Washington.

ED: Oh yeah? My mom got her Ph.D at U-Dub.

TULSA: *(Surprised)* Really?

ED: *(Sarcastically)* Oh yeah. I'm only the first generation to express the illiterate T V actor gene in my family. My parents, and many of my ancestors, could actually read.

TULSA: I didn't mean that.

ED: I know. I'm oversensitive to other peoples' perception of me. *(Beat)* That, in fact, is my job description. Was.

TULSA: Was?

ED: I quit my show two days ago and left town with my backpack. So, I'm afraid you'll have to catch it in reruns.

TULSA: Why'd you quit?

ED: Because I'm not a boy anymore. I'm thirty.

(TULSA looks at ED.)

ED: Ya know?

(Blackout)

I.11
BUSTED FLAT IN BABYLON

(Lights discover Senator MELVIN PIKE.*)*

MELVIN: My fellow Americans, I'm talking about
Security. *(Beat)* Security of the Homeland. The Security
of the women, men, and children of this great Nation.
The Security of the Ideals, Concepts, Precepts, and
Doctrines that bind Us together as a People. There
are those who would threaten Us and all We stand for.
Who would use Terror to undermine Our Freedom
and destroy Our Way of Life. But I say to these Infidels,
these Hostile Combatants who plot with evil minds and
Godless hearts to rob Us of Our Security; I say to them:
"Nuh-uh." *(Beat)* My fellow Americans, the time has
come to identify the Enemy. And that doesn't just mean
the Terrorist with his foreign names and gods and
customs, who hates and despises with every fiber of his
being all that is Good and Pure and True in Us. Oh no,
my friends. That Enemy is well known, and make
no mistake; We will find him and We will deal with
him severely. *(Beat)* But an even greater Enemy exists
among Us. It might be you. It might be him. It might
be her. The Enemy is anyone who dares, in any way,
to question the validity, or impede the progress, of Our
Righteous Cause. *(Beat)* My fellow Americans, make no
mistake. If you value your Security, you will be with
Us and not against Us. But should you dare to exercise
the Freedoms of this Great Land without pledging
Allegiance to the Government and the One True God
from which those Freedoms derive... you're gonna find
yourself in a world of hurt. *(Beat)* God Bless America.

(Lights discover BOB.*)*

BOB: This was last speech made by former war hero, Senator Melvin Pike, Republican, of Idaho, before the United States Senate. September 13th, 2001. The Senator spoke in support of a piece of legislation known as The Preservation of American Freedom and Security Act. The bill, written by Senator Pike himself, proposed, among other things, permanent military control of the government; closure of all U S borders; repeal of Amendments one through twelve; an immediate end to funding for public education; the abolition of the arts; and moving the nation's capitol to an underground bunker outside Boise. *(Beat)* When this measure was defeated by a vote of ninety-nine to one, Senator Pike abandoned his congressional career and continued his crusade in other areas...

(Haunting organ music starts. ROSE and VALERIE enter. MELVIN re-appears in the costume and attitude of an evangelical zealot. He addresses his congregation. ROSE and VALERIE kneel and listen.)

MELVIN: Brothers and Sisters, we are living in the Final Days.

(Coyotes growl and wail.)

MELVIN: The unwashed and unholy steal the air that would fill our lungs and the lungs of our righteous children. The vile stench of the great whore America hangs heavy on the ill wind that blows above the heads of our blessed children as they sleep. We are living in the Final Days.

(Music surges. Coyotes howl.)

MELVIN: We are busted flat in Babylon!

(Suddenly, everything freezes. Lights discover TULSA and ED in the car. TULSA has just switched off the radio broadcast of MELVIN's sermon.)

TULSA: Oh my God, I can't stand that guy.

(TULSA *and* ED *drive on in silence.* MELVIN *unfreezes and continues with his sermon.*)

MELVIN: Now is the time of vengeance, yea, vengeance upon the evil doers and enemies of thine God! Now is not the time for the turning of cheeks. The last cheek hath turned. Now is the time for cheek and jowl and wretched, sinful tongue alike to be cut from the heads of the unwashed and unholy. Now is the time of vengeance! (*He freezes.*)

ED: So what's your major?

(TULSA *frowns.*)

ED: What? Was that lame?

TULSA: No. I'm writing a doctoral thesis on Bob Dylan. (*Beat*) That's lame.

ED: I don't know. (*Singing the line, a la Dylan*) "I think it sounds kinda cool."

(TULSA *sighs.*)

ED: I bet people do that to you a lot, don't they?

TULSA: Yeah.

ED: Sorry.

(TULSA *laughs to herself. They make eye contact, smile at one another briefly, then* TULSA *looks back at the road. Lights fade on* ED *and* TULSA. MELVIN *unfreezes.*)

MELVIN: Now is the time for blood to spill. In the name of our one true God and for the sake of our righteous, blessed children.

(*Music swells. Coyotes wail.*)

MELVIN: WE ARE LIVING IN THE FINAL DAYS! AND NOW IS THE TIME TO SEND THE DEVIL BACK HIS OWN!

(*Two Treasury* AGENTS *storm the stage with rifles.*)

AGENT #1: Freeze!

(ROSE *and* VALERIE *scream. Off-stage, the coyotes go insane.*)

MELVIN: (*To congregation*) Behold! The attack dogs of the Great Whore Babylon!

AGENT #2: Melvin Pike, you are under arrest by authority of the United States Treasury Department.

AGENT #1: Put your hands above your head!

(*As soon as* MELVIN *begins to slowly move one hand, the* AGENTS *gun him down in a hail of bullets.* ROSE *and* VALERIE *scream.*)

(*Blackout*)

I.12
CLYDE SNIFFS THE AIR AND TRAVELS WESTWARD

(*Lights discover* CLYDE *alone in his combine.*)

(*He steps down to the ground and looks in all directions. He stoops to the ground and sniffs. He stands, throws his head back, and sniffs the air. He decides upon a direction, then hops back in the combine.*)

(*Lights fade.*)

I.13
NO CARS

(TULSA *stands outside a rental car place.* ED *walks up to her, a brochure in his hand. He shrugs.*)

ED: No cars.

TULSA: None?

ED: Nope. Lady at the counter said they haven't had any for a couple of days. Apparently everyone rents them to leave.

TULSA: What are you going to do?

ED: Well, she gave me the names of a couple of motels and put my name on a list. I figure I'll just hang out here till they get one in. What about you? Heading on?

TULSA: Yeah. I think I better.

ED: Sure.

TULSA: So, what's next for you?

(ED *shows her the brochure.*)

TULSA: "World's Largest Hand-Dug Well."

ED: It says here it's actually so big you could put the world's largest ball of twine inside it. Twice.

TULSA: Sounds great.

ED: *(Extending his hand)* Listen, thanks again for the ride. I think you probably saved my life.

TULSA: You would've done the same for me.

ED: But you wouldn't have been running from antelope.

(They both laugh.)

TULSA: True.

ED: Take care, Tulsa. I hope everything goes all right. And I'm sorry about your mom.

TULSA: Thanks. *(Beat)* Ed?

ED: *(Turning)* Yeah.

TULSA: You wanna drive to Oklahoma with me?

ED: *(Ripping brochure in half)* Love to.

(Blackout)

I.14
ROSE AND VALERIE HIT THE ROAD

(Lights discover ROSE *and* VALERIE *standing by the road, trying to hitch-hike.)*

VALERIE: Do you see anything, Rose?

ROSE: *(Aggravated)* Do you see anything, Valerie?

VALERIE: No.

ROSE: Then I don't see anything.

VALERIE: Where are we going?

ROSE: We're not going anywhere, Valerie. We're standing beside the road.

VALERIE: If we get a ride, I mean.

ROSE: I don't know.

VALERIE: We won't get very far without any money. We never got a chance to steal Father Melvin's when those G-men came.

ROSE: I realize that, Valerie.

VALERIE: I think we should go see Bob.

ROSE: No.

VALERIE: He'll help us, Rosie.

*(*ROSE *doesn't answer. They are both distracted by the rattling sound of an approaching vehicle.)*

ROSE: What the hell is that?

*(*CLYDE *enters, crawling on all fours and sniffing the ground. He looks up at* ROSE *and* VALERIE.*)*

CLYDE: Y'all need a ride?

*(*ROSE *and* VALERIE *nod. Blackout)*

I.15
LATER

(Lights discover TULSA *and* ED *in the car. It's near dawn.*
ED *is driving.* TULSA *is asleep, having a bad dream.* ED
*starts to nod off, then jerks back awake. Music plays softly
on the car stereo.)*

(Lights discover SYLVIA *wandering, disoriented, beside the
road. She holds the baby Tulsa in her arms.* TULSA's *reaction
lets us know that she is dreaming this.)*

SYLVIA: *(Frantic)* Woody! Woody, where are you?
Woody! Where are you?

TULSA: MOM!

*(*TULSA *screams, waking* ED *who has fallen asleep and veered
over the center line.)*

(Lights fade on SYLVIA.*)*

(SFX: Brakes screeching)

(The sound of the tires skidding wakes TULSA, *who leaps for
the wheel, and ends up in* ED's *arms as they come to a stop.)*

(They are both charged with adrenaline. TULSA *looks at* ED
*and suddenly kisses him. The impulsive kiss slowly grows
more passionate, then just as quickly,* TULSA *pulls away from
him.)*

(They sit in stunned, awkward silence.)

(Lights fade.)

I.16
THE LONELINESS OF THE LONG DISTANCE FARMER

(ROSE *and* VALERIE *are with* CLYDE *in the combine.* CLYDE *tries to conceal the fact that he is crying.*)

VALERIE: Are you all right?

(CLYDE *nods, sniffs tears.*)

VALERIE: You want some tissue?

(CLYDE *shakes his head, wipes his nose on his sleeve.*)

VALERIE: You sure you don't wanna talk about it, Clyde?

(CLYDE *shakes his head "no."*)

VALERIE: Might make you feel better.

ROSE: What'd you do to her, Jethro?

(CLYDE *cries harder.*)

ROSE: Lie to her?

(CLYDE *sniffs, shakes his head.*)

ROSE: Goin around behind her back?

(CLYDE *cries, shakes his head.*)

ROSE: Push her around like the big stupid monkey that you are?

(CLYDE *wails, shakes his head in the affirmative.*)

VALERIE: Rose, stop picking on him.

ROSE: He deserves it. Don't you, Gomer?

(CLYDE *agrees, cries some more.*)

ROSE: Bet you're sorry now, aren't you?

(CLYDE *nods.*)

ROSE: Yep. You always are once it's too late.

VALERIE: Here, honey. Take this.

(VALERIE *offers him a tissue.* CLYDE *takes it and blows his nose loudly.*)

CLYDE: (*Choking back tears*) Thank you.

(*Blackout*) .

I.17
REGISTRATION

(MISS NEBRASKA *stands in* BOB's *office with her shotgun.* BOB *listens intently and with compassion as she tells him her story.*)

MISS NEBRASKA: And then he grabbed me and drug me right off the stage. Right there in front of the chaperones and the judges and Regis and everybody. I've never been so embarrassed in my entire life.

(BOB *gently takes the gun away from her and puts it behind the counter as he speaks.*)

BOB: Miss Nebraska, I am so sorry. I am sure that you would've won the Miss America title.

MISS NEBRASKA: Really?

BOB: There is no doubt in my mind.

MISS NEBRASKA: I just don't know what I'm going to do, Bill.

BOB: Bob.

MISS NEBRASKA: Bob.

BOB: Well, first of all, tonight you'll stay here.

MISS NEBRASKA: But I don't have any money.

BOB: Forget about money. You told me your story. This is payment enough.

MISS NEBRASKA: I couldn't do that.

BOB: Of course you could. *(He hands her a registration form.)* It is as simple as filling out this piece of paper. You'll repay me when you're famous.

MISS NEBRASKA: Thank you.

(MISS NEBRASKA starts to fill out the form. TULSA and ED enter.)

BOB: Greetings travelers!

TULSA: Hello.

MISS NEBRASKA: *(To TULSA)* Hi.

ED: *(To BOB)* How's it going?

BOB: Well, the sun is shining, my lungs are breathing and people are coming through the door to rent my rooms. It is, I would say, not bad. Are you together?

TULSA: No. Two rooms please.

(BOB gives them registration forms as he speaks.)

BOB: Very well, then. As I was just telling this lovely young lady here, there is a very ancient custom here at Bob's American Motel of writing information about yourself on pieces of paper when renting a room. So if you each would please take a pen and see that this ritual continues, I will appreciate that.

TULSA: Are you Bob?

BOB: Yes. That is me.

TULSA: I'm Tulsa Lovechild.

BOB: *(Recognizing her name)* Oh my goodness! Is this true? *(He shakes her hand and laughs.)* Little Tulsa Lovechild standing here in front of me! All grown up!

Look at you. Beautiful girl. *(To* MISS NEBRASKA *and ED)*
This girl, I am here the night she is born. Swear to God.
No lie. Room twenty-three. Her mother calls the front
desk, pregnant, "Omigosh, I'm having my baby!"
I panic. Craziness. Insanity. And then, Tulsa Lovechild
is born right there in front of me. Literally knocked my
socks off.

TULSA: It's good to finally meet you.

BOB: Oh, it is my pleasure.

TULSA: This is, uh, my friend. Ed Caribou.

(BOB and ED shake hands.)

BOB: Edward.

ED: Nice to meet you.

BOB: You look familiar to me.

MISS NEBRASKA: *(Finally placing him)* Yes! You're the
guy from the T V aren't you?

ED: *(Introducing himself)* Edward Caribou.

MISS NEBRASKA: Right. You play that Buckshot fella.

ED: Johnny Buckskin.

MISS NEBRASKA: Right.

TULSA: Boy Detective.

MISS NEBRASKA: What is that you always say?
"Hold on, there's somethin' else!"

ED: But wait! There's more!

MISS NEBRASKA: Yeah. Something like that. Boy,
it's a real pleasure to meet you. *(She shakes his hand.)*
I'm Kelli Jo Daugherty. I'm a real big fan of your show.

ED: Thank you.

MISS NEBRASKA: *(To* TULSA*)* I'm sorry. What was your
name again?

TULSA: Tulsa Lovechild.

(MISS NEBRASKA *shakes* TULSA's *hand.*)

MISS NEBRASKA: Well, I'll be darned. That's a funny name.

TULSA: Yeah. Wacky Indians.

(MISS NEBRASKA *experiences a moment of confusion, but it passes.*)

MISS NEBRASKA: Are you an actor too?

TULSA: No. I'm just a person.

MISS NEBRASKA: Oh.

TULSA: Excuse me.

(TULSA *crosses to* BOB *at the counter.*)

BOB: How is your mother?

(TULSA *looks at him and starts to cry.* BOB *comforts her.*)

BOB: There, there sweet girl. I am sorry.

MISS NEBRASKA: (*Obliviously, to* ED) So, are you shootin' a movie down here or something?

(*Blackout*)

I.18
A FAREWELL TO CLYDE

(*Lights discover* CLYDE *as he is letting* ROSE *and* VALERIE *out of the combine.*)

CLYDE: I really wanna thank you both for talkin' to me. Boy, I really feel a lot better.

ROSE: Sure. Thanks for the ride.

CLYDE: You bet.

VALERIE: Thanks for everything, Clyde.

CLYDE: Good-bye now. Good luck with your operation.

(CLYDE *offers them a big, warm hug.* ROSE *tries to dodge it, but* VALERIE *accepts.*)

VALERIE: Thank you. Goodbye Clyde.

CLYDE: You ladies take care of yourselves.

VALERIE: You too.

CLYDE: I will.

VALERIE: You promise?

CLYDE: Yes ma'am.

ROSE: Okay. That should do it. (*She breaks out of the hug.*)

VALERIE: Love yourself, Clyde.

CLYDE: Yes ma'am. You too, Miss Valerie. Goodbye Miss Rose.

ROSE: You bet.

(CLYDE *watches them exit. Once they are gone, he smells something in the air. He tracks the scent to the edge of the stage where he discovers* MISS NEBRASKA's *banner lying on the ground. He picks up the banner and sniffs, then looks in the distance toward the motel.*)

(*Blackout*)

I.19
REUNION

(*Lights discover* BOB *behind the counter.* ROSE *and* VALERIE *enter.*)

ROSE: Hi.

BOB: Hello.

VALERIE: Hi, Bob.

BOB: Hello Valerie.

(BOB *kisses* VALERIE *on the cheek.* ROSE *and* BOB *look at one another uncertainly.*)

VALERIE: Oh, for Heaven's sake, all right.

(VALERIE *turns her head and closes her eyes.* BOB *kisses* ROSE *passionately on the mouth.*)

(*Blackout*)

I.20
ROMANCE BLOOMS AT EXIT 238

(*Lights discover* TULSA *outside her motel room with the urn.* ED *approaches.*)

ED: Hi.

TULSA: Hi.

ED: How are you?

TULSA: I'm okay.

ED: How long has it been?

TULSA: I beg your pardon?

ED: Your mother.

TULSA: Three weeks. She was sick for a while though.

ED: I can't imagine.

TULSA: I can't either. (*Explaining*) I wasn't around. She was dying in Bozeman and I was in Seattle. Hiding. I didn't see her at all for the last three months. (*With a self-deprecating laugh*) I don't do Death well. Or life for that matter. But other than that... (*Beat*) I mean, staying with your mother while she dies. Isn't that one of those things you're supposed to have an instinct for?

ED: I don't know. I don't think I've ever done anything by instinct. Most of the moments of my life pass while I'm preparing for them.

(TULSA *and* ED *notice* CLYDE *crawling across the parking lot, sniffing the ground.*)

CLYDE: Hey.

TULSA & ED: Hey.

(TULSA *and* ED *laugh as* CLYDE *moves on.*)

ED: I'm sorry about earlier in the car.

TULSA: Why are you sorry? I'm the one who kissed you.

ED: Well, my lips were there too. They're not innocent. (TULSA *laughs.*) I'm sorry because I enjoyed talking with you a lot.

TULSA: Thanks. Me too. *(Beat)* I must seem incredibly strange to you.

ED: I've spent the last twenty years in a town where people have psychics for their pets. The word "strange" no longer has any connotative value for me.

TULSA: I'm developing quite an admiration for your vocabulary.

ED: What if I were to say that the feeling is incontrovertibly mutual?

TULSA: I expected you to be chasing after Miss Genetic Perfection by now.

ED: Why would you assume that?

TULSA: Oh, I don't know. Natural pessimism affirmed almost unanimously by experience.

ED: I like a woman who appreciates me for my mind.

TULSA: You know, you're nothing at all like I would've imagined you to be. I mean, if I had actually known who you were before we met.

(ED *kisses her.*)

ED: Did you ever imagine something like that would happen?

TULSA: Actually, it was more like this.

(TULSA *kisses him.*)

ED: Tulsa, is this okay?

TULSA: Well, it's not your typical boy-meets-girl scenario. But what the hell.

(*They kiss again.*)

I.21
A QUIET MOMENT OF TURNPIKE SERENITY

(*Lights stay up on* TULSA *and* ED *as we discover* BOB *sitting with twins, looking at the stars.*)

(*Lights rise on* CLYDE, *who kneels on a hill just up the road from the motel.*)

BOB: (*To audience*) I write to my mother in Moscow, try to explain the peacefulness of the interstate at night. She does not understand. What peace, she says? Still the cars, they go all night, yes? It is never hearing the engines running smoothly in the cooler air of the evening. Makes her fail to get it. The comforting sound of constant motion. Overhearing the whisper of Today saying to Tomorrow, "Hello again there. How are you?" Trading moon for sun, they smile at a million new stories the one has to tell the other. I smile too. Never quite sure, if they know I'm listening.

(As lights begin to fade, CLYDE *throws back his head and sends a mournful, lovesick howl toward the moon.)*

END OF ACT ONE

ACT TWO:
ALL YOU CAN EAT

II.01
LONG TIME GONE

(Light appears D S C. Two Army MEDICS *carry* WOODY
in on a stretcher and leave him. He has been wounded.
His uniform is torn and he is covered with blood. The sound
of helicopters in the distance gradually fades as WOODY
speaks to the audience.)

WOODY: Some of us in the platoon used to speculate
about the afterlife. Whether or not there was such a
thing and what it was like. Not that we were really a
metaphysically minded bunch of people. It's just that
the circumstances of our daily lives at the time sort of
inspired consideration of the question.
One guy, Junior, from Missouri thought it would be
like spending forever on the Lake of the Ozarks,
catching fish every time he threw his line into the water.
Spud, from New York City, thought of Death as an
eternal taxi ride through mid-town.
I didn't know what to think, so I just imagined being
stoned forever. An endless loop of barely coherent,
but seemingly profound, thoughts and insights flashing
across my mind to the background beat of a warm,
pleasant hum. Not a spiritually ambitious idea. But
it worked for me.
Only thing was, I turned out to be absolutely dead
wrong. If you'll pardon the pun.

You know what it's like? Believe me, I've had some
time to think about this and I think I've come up with
the perfect analogy. It's like being on one of those game
shows where they put you in the soundproof booth.
Forever.

At first I wondered what was going to happen to me
next. Good old Western linear thinking. Automatically
assuming there was a "next." A concept I've since
abandoned. Now I just wonder.

I think about Vietnam. How many more corpses piled
up behind mine? I wonder if anybody ever figured out
a reason for it that they could live with.

I think about what I saw on television my last morning
as a civilian. Those kids, terrified and bleeding in
Grant Park. I wonder what kind of world they woke
up to when those wounds healed. If they healed. The
movement that Sylvia believed in so passionately. All
those dreamers. I wonder if any of it survived.

I think about Sylvia. I wonder if she ever forgave me
for what I did. Did she know that I too thought it was
pointless and cowardly? And that I loved her.

I think about our child. What kind of world does my
son or daughter live in? I wonder if he or she ever plays
my eight-tracks. Or think of me? Feel how much I wish
I'd known him? Or her.

That's what it's like.

(Lights fade on WOODY. MEDICS *return and carry him
away.)*

II.02
RESURRECTION

*(The organ music from the earlier compound scene is recalled
with a slight echo effect as* ROSE *and* VALERIE *are discovered
in bed, in the throes of a nightmare.)*

(As their sleep grows more troubled, a red light appears beneath the bed. ROSE and VALERIE toss and turn as the light grows brighter.)

(Two hands emerge from beneath the bed and grasp the frame. MELVIN pulls himself out from under the bed and slowly rises to his feet. He's dressed in a business suit and carries a briefcase.)

(MELVIN cleans himself off. He crosses D S C and checks himself out in an invisible mirror. He combs his hair, checks his teeth, straightens his tie, winks at himself in the mirror.)

(MELVIN turns to face ROSE and VALERIE. At the same moment, their nightmare reaches its climax. They both wake up screaming when they see MELVIN. MELVIN looks at them. He smiles, turns, exits. Lights fade.)

II.03
MORNING

(Lights discover BOB strolling through the motel parking lot with a cup of coffee.)

BOB: Good morning. This is a moment I also enjoy. Just before the sun rises over the exit ramp and calls the travelers back to the road. Soon there will be children to be dressed, cars to be packed, maps to be consulted. But for now there is only this. A cup of coffee. And the feeling of beginning. *(He takes a drink of coffee.)* Mm. This is good.

(Lights fade.)

II.04
SEX AND POLITICS

(Lights discover TULSA *and* ED *in bed.* ED *wakes up to find her dressed and sitting on the edge of the bed.)*

ED: Good morning.

TULSA: So I would officially be a tabloid headline at this point, right?

ED: Potentially. Yes. Congratulations.

TULSA: Thanks. *(Beat)* Ed?

ED: Yeah?

TULSA: You don't have to answer this....

ED: Okay...

TULSA: But who did you vote for in the last election?

ED: What?

TULSA: You really don't have to answer.

ED: I voted for Gore. Why?

TULSA: I've never slept with anyone without knowing who they voted for.

(ED laughs.)

TULSA: Is that funny?

ED: What do you do, take a poll?

TULSA: What I mean is I usually know something about them.

ED: What are you talking about? I told you my whole life story in the car. More than you told me about you, actually.

TULSA: Well, gee Ed, I guess you won the exposition contest.

ED: *(Starts getting dressed)* That's not what I meant.

TULSA: I like to know what I feel about someone before I'm intimate with them. Is that such a foreign concept to you?

ED: Contrary to your assumption, no, it isn't.

TULSA: I'm not assuming anything.

ED: So, I suppose it would have changed how you feel about me if I told you I voted for Bush instead.

TULSA: Of course it would have.

ED: Okay, so how do you feel about me knowing that I voted for Gore?

TULSA: I feel...not surprised.

ED: Not surprised?

TULSA: I'm not surprised.

ED: Is that good?

TULSA: It's not bad.

ED: All right. Can I play too? Who did you vote for?

TULSA: I didn't vote.

ED: What?

TULSA: I didn't vote.

ED: You're kidding me!

TULSA: Does that surprise you?

ED: Yes. Of course it does.

TULSA: Of course?

ED: It surprises me.

TULSA: Why?

ED: Because you seem...like someone who would vote.
I mean, you talk about the sixties and everything—

TULSA: So that means I vote?

ED: I would think so. Normally. Yes.

TULSA: Ed, in all the time we drove together, we didn't
have a single discussion of what either of us believes
in politically. We talked but we didn't come anywhere
near learning anything meaningful about each other.
It was journalism, Ed. We reported to each other on
selected events of our lives, with a few commercial
breaks to plug our personal obsessions and favorite
books. Then we cut to the sex scene.

ED: Well Jesus Christ, Tulsa. It was only nine hundred
fucking miles! I suppose if we'd been driving to Tierra
Del Fuego and back, maybe we might've had time
to unlock the boundless secrets of each other's souls
before we went to bed together. But I think at the very
least we can safely say that it was a little more than
dinner and a movie!

TULSA: You don't have to yell.

ED: I don't mean to. I'm sorry. I just thought that last
night was—

TULSA: Was what?

ED: I thought it was all right.

TULSA: All right?

ED: No, it was great. What I mean is, I thought we were
cleared for take-off.

TULSA: Cleared for take-off? Tell me you didn't just say
that.

ED: I don't know how else to say it. I thought it was
okay with you that we had sex. Together.

TULSA: Well, of course it was or it wouldn't have happened.

ED: Well ... then I don't understand what we're fighting about.

TULSA: We're not fighting. We're having a discussion.

ED: About?

TULSA: Context.

ED: Oh. *(Fully clothed now, he moves away from the bed.)*

TULSA: Where are you going?

ED: I'm not going anywhere.

TULSA: You were walking toward the door.

ED: I'm pacing.

TULSA: Why are you pacing?

ED: I'm hungry. I thought about getting some breakfast.

TULSA: So that would be it for you then?

ED: Maybe a paper.

TULSA: Don't try to be funny right now, please.

ED: What would you like me to say?

TULSA: I have no idea what I would like you to say. I've just been preparing myself to react to whatever it is you do say.

ED: Tulsa, can I ask you something?

TULSA: What?

ED: Do you feel under any obligation to be unhappy?

(Beat)

TULSA: I don't think so.

ED: So why don't we go to breakfast?

TULSA: And what will that mean?

ED: Toast most likely. Definitely some coffee. And there may also be a possibility of eggs.

TULSA: Sure. Why not? No sense facing the grisly end on an empty stomach, right?

ED: Please don't feel like you have to suppress your cynicism on my account. It's the essence of your charm.

TULSA: Your sarcasm is equally appealing.

(They start toward the door.)

ED: *(Stopping)* So why didn't you vote?

TULSA: Does it matter?

ED: I like to know something about people before I go to breakfast with them.

TULSA: It felt like applying for disappointment.

(ED nods.)

TULSA: Sort of like this.

(TULSA exits. Blackout)

II.05
MISS NEBRASKA PHONES THE PROPER AUTHORITIES

(Lights up on MISS NEBRASKA in her motel room. She dials the phone and waits for a response.)

MISS NEBRASKA: Hello? Is this the F B I? This is Kelli Jo Daugherty. Miss Nebraska. *(Beat)* I was just calling to let y'all know that my boyfriend Clyde, Clyde Nicholson, didn't kidnap me, okay? *(Beat)* No. It was just a misunderstanding. Everything's all right now. *(Beat)* Don't arrest him or anything, okay? *(Beat)* Thank you. Bye. *(She hangs up the phone. She picks it back up and*

dials another number.) Mom? Hi. It's Kelli. *(Fighting tears)*
Oh, I'm all right. How are you doin'?

(Blackout)

II.06
BEWARE THE WRATH OF THE APPALACHIAN HALF-MAN

(Lights up on BOB, ROSE *and* VALERIE *in the office.)*

BOB: It was a very long time that I didn't hear anything from you.

VALERIE: Things went badly with the carnival.

BOB: How do you mean?

VALERIE: There was a boy named Danny who traveled with the show. He used to help us carry our bags into the room when we stopped here. Do you remember him?

BOB: Yes. He was a good kid. Very ugly.

VALERIE: His stage name was Danny the Dog-Faced Boy. He worked with us in the Natural Wonders exhibit.

ROSE: The term is freak show, sister.

VALERIE: You can call it that if you want but I prefer to think of myself as a natural wonder. *(To* BOB*)* The barker used to say that Danny was part boy and part dog but that really wasn't true.

ROSE: As far as we know.

VALERIE: He had peculiar features. And an unusual abundance of facial hair. But he had the sweetest eyes.

ROSE: And a cute little cold nose.

VALERIE: *(A mild warning)* Rose. *(To* BOB*)* Danny got into some trouble with the man who ran the natural Wonders exhibit. You remember Cyrus.

BOB: The Appalachian Half Man. Yes.

VALERIE: Danny was in love with Cyrus' wife.

ROSE: He was mounting the Yak Lady.

VALERIE: Must you always express everything in the crudest terms possible?

ROSE: Well, that's what happened, isn't it? No sense trying to put a better face on it. So to speak.

VALERIE: *(Upset)* Now, Rose, you stop that. I mean it. *(To* BOB*)* Cyrus killed him. He shot him dead right there in front of all of us.

*(*VALERIE *is upset.* ROSE *takes her hand.)*

ROSE: *(To* BOB*)* Valerie was too upset to stay with the carnival. We both were. We left. But Cyrus blackballed us. We couldn't work with any of the shows on the circuit. And there weren't a lot of job openings that we were qualified for.

VALERIE: That's when we met Father Melvin.

ROSE: And continued our string of bad moves.

BOB: Why didn't you come to me?

ROSE: I thought about it.

VALERIE: I wanted to.

*(*ROSE *squeezes* VALERIE*'s hand.)*

VALERIE: Ow!

ROSE: *(To* BOB*)* I was afraid that you wouldn't want me around for more than a week at a time. *(Beat)* I was also afraid that you would.

BOB: I would have helped you.

ROSE: Would you still? There's a doctor in Los Angeles who performs a new operation that might help Valerie and me. Separate us.

BOB: This is excellent news. Isn't it?

VALERIE: We're talking a lot of money, Bob.

BOB: How much?

ROSE: A lot.

(Lights fade.)

II.07
RECONCILIATION, TAKE 1

(MISS NEBRASKA is discovered in her room, still on the phone with her mother.)

MISS NEBRASKA: Oh yeah. You wouldn't believe what a nice guy Regis really is in person. He treated everybody just like we were old friends. He didn't seem stuck up at all. Yeah. I thought that was nice too.

(CLYDE enters. He knocks on her door.)

MISS NEBRASKA: Hold on, Mom. *(Covers the phone)* Who is it?

(CLYDE knocks again.)

MISS NEBRASKA: Just a minute, Mom. I'll be right back. *(She sets the phone down and crosses to the door.)*

CLYDE: Kelli Jo.

MISS NEBRASKA: How did you find me?

CLYDE: I don't know how. I just did.

MISS NEBRASKA: Well, I don't wanna see you.

CLYDE: Honey—

MISS NEBRASKA: Don't make me scream bloody murder and get the cops here after you, Clyde.

CLYDE: I want to apologize.

MISS NEBRASKA: You do, huh?

CLYDE: Yeah.

MISS NEBRASKA: Well, go ahead. Apologize.

CLYDE: I thought I just did.

MISS NEBRASKA: That was it?

CLYDE: Yeah.

MISS NEBRASKA: You done apologizing now?

CLYDE: I reckon.

MISS NEBRASKA: Good.

(MISS NEBRASKA *punches* CLYDE. *He falls to the floor. She holds her hand.*)

MISS NEBRASKA: Shit! (*Picks up phone*) Hello, Mom? You still there? I'm gonna have to call you back, all right? Okay. I'll talk to you later. Love ya.

(MISS NEBRASKA *hangs up the phone. She stares at* CLYDE.)

(*Blackout*)

II.08
FAMILIAL TENSION; OR THE POLITICS OF BREAKFAST

(TULSA *and* ED *walk into a diner near the motel.* TULSA *sees* SYLVIA *and* STOCKTON, *circa 1991, sitting at a table.* STOCKTON *is working on a healthy stack of pancakes.* SYLVIA *has a bowl of fruit.* ED *doesn't see them as he and* TULSA *sit on the other side of the same table.*)

ED: What's wrong?

TULSA: Nothing.

(ED *looks at the menu.*)

STOCKTON: Gulf War, my ass. It's 1991. There's no comparison to Vietnam. The whole thing will be over in a week.

TULSA: The whole thing is bullshit.

STOCKTON: Of course it is. This country runs on bullshit.

TULSA: There's no reason we should be fighting a war over there.

STOCKTON: *(Sardonically)* Don't you watch the news? We're defending Democracy.

TULSA: We're defending oil companies.

STOCKTON: *(Baiting her)* That's not what George said.

TULSA: George is a fascist.

STOCKTON: George Bush wouldn't make a good pimple on a fascist's ass.

TULSA: It's just wrong.

STOCKTON: *(Amused)* Well, why don't you call up your President and tell him. He might not have thought of that.

TULSA: He's not my president. I didn't vote for him.

STOCKTON: That's right. You didn't. And if you don't vote, you don't bitch.

TULSA: And if you do vote you share the blame.

STOCKTON: Hippie talk.

SYLVIA: Stockton.

STOCKTON: We know where she gets that.

SYLVIA: *(To STOCKTON)* Eat your pancakes.

TULSA: *(To* SYLVIA*)* You're strangely quiet on this matter, comrade.

SYLVIA: I just hope those boys are safe.

ED: You know what you want?

TULSA: *(Drawn back)* What?

ED: What are you gonna have?

TULSA: Oh. *(Looks at* SYLVIA*'s plate)* Fruit.

ED: I think I'm gonna go for the pancakes.

*(*TULSA *does a double take between* STOCKTON *and* ED*.)*

ED: You all right?

TULSA: Fine. You?

ED: Good.

TULSA: Good.

SYLVIA: *(To* TULSA*)* Have there been protests?

TULSA: What?

SYLVIA: On campus.

TULSA: A few.

SYLVIA: Did you get involved?

TULSA: Y'know, Mom, I just couldn't decide between that and the homecoming committee.

SYLVIA: I just asked if you'd participated. You obviously have opinions about it.

TULSA: I think half the people are only doing it because in their head they look really cool to themselves. It all seems a little contrived.

STOCKTON: Hippie theatrics. Always been that way. Your mother can tell you.

SYLVIA: I protested the war because I thought it was wrong. Not to be on T V.

TULSA: Well, Mom, I'm afraid the times they have a-changed.

(ED *stands.*)

ED: Will you excuse me for a minute?

TULSA: What's wrong?

ED: Nothing. I'll be right back.

TULSA: Okay.

(TULSA *watches* ED *exit.*)

STOCKTON: We nailed another one of their weapons plants last night.

TULSA: *(Sarcastically)* Go Team!

SYLVIA: *(Admonishing her)* Tulsa.

STOCKTON: I watched the whole thing on C N N.

TULSA: Of course.

STOCKTON: I taped it if you wanna see it.

TULSA: Great. Maybe later we can pop some popcorn and dig out that old Super Eight footage of the My Lai massacre.

SYLVIA: Tulsa, that isn't funny!

STOCKTON: *(Angrily, to* TULSA*)* Who the hell do you think you are?

SYLVIA: Stockton—

STOCKTON: No, I wanna know where this girl gets all her moral superiority. *(To* TULSA*)* D'you take a class for that?

SYLVIA: Stockton, please.

STOCKTON: *(To* TULSA*)* If you and all your hippie friends know so much about how the world oughta be, why don't you shut your damn mouths and go do something about it?

TULSA: Go to Hell.

SYLVIA: Stop it! Both of you.

TULSA: *(Standing)* Sorry, Mom. I don't have to take this shit. I'm not the one who married him.

*(*TULSA *storms out.* SYLVIA *gives* STOCKTON *an angry look, then follows* TULSA*.)*

*(*STOCKTON *shakes his head, wipes his mouth, then addresses the audience.)*

STOCKTON: I continue to use the term "hippies" as a nostalgic impulse, although it is no longer technically correct. As of 1980. Early '81 if you're splitting hairs. Since that time there have actually been no more authentic hippies living in the wild, so to speak. It was Reagan's idea, although like with most of the other jobs, the Master Thespian was careful not to get his own hands dirty. It was one of my last gigs with the agency. We rounded them all up, from Frisco to Ann Arbor, Santa Fe to Woodstock. Marched 'em with their bongs and sandals and scratched-up copies of the White Album, down to a minimum security holding compound way out on one of the far corners of Barry Goldwater's ranch in Arizona. You may think you see some left-over flower children here and there, mostly around your college campuses and small Western cities. But those are our people.

(Lights fade.)

II.09
HAMLET, PRINCE OF HOLLYWOOD

(ED *is discovered at a pay phone. He dials a number just as* BOB *enters.*)

BOB: Now I think I've finally figured out where I've seen you before.

ED: Yeah, I know. I'm on television, remember?

BOB: T V? No. I don't watch T V.

ED: Right.

BOB: Hamlet.

ED: Excuse me?

BOB: That's where I saw you. Hamlet.

ED: You saw my Hamlet?

BOB: Indeed.

ED: But that was in California.

BOB: Yes. It was at the same time as the annual convention of the Motel Owners of North America. MONA, as we say. February 1996, yes?

ED: That's right! I'll be damned. So, uh, what'd you think?

BOB: Magnificent.

ED: No kidding. You really liked it?

BOB: It was the best Hamlet I ever saw.

ED: Thank you. I really appreciate—

(*Lights up on* STANLEY, *who enters wearing leather pants, mask, and nipple clamps, holding a phone.*)

STANLEY: Hello?

ED: *(To* BOB*)* Excuse me. *(Into phone)* Stanley?

STANLEY: Ed?

ED: Hi.

STANLEY: Ed, where are you?

ED: I'm on the road.

STANLEY: Where are you? Vegas?

ED: I'm in Oklahoma, Stanley.

STANLEY: Holy Christ, Ed. I don't even know where that is. What are you doing there?

ED: *(Sarcastically)* It's right next to Indiana.

STANLEY: Son-of-a-bitch, Ed, what are you doing in the South?

ED: Stanley, I met a woman.

STANLEY: Oh fuck me.

ED: Her name's Tulsa Lovechild.

STANLEY: Ed, listen to me, okay buddy? This is Stanley talking to you. I want you to take a little piece of advice. Lose the stripper and get your ass back here. I've got something important to talk to you about.

ED: Stanley, you perverse bastard, it's not like that.

STANLEY: Perverse? Where do you get off calling me perverse, pal?

ED: She's not a stripper. She's great, Stanley. I think I really like her.

STANLEY: *(Sarcastically)* That's really sweet, Ed.

ED: I've never met anyone like her.

STANLEY: Well, hot diggity. Congratulations, Ed. Listen, I hope you and this girl have a really nice time out there in Indiana planting the crops and raising the barn and fucking the goddamn sheep or whatever the fuck else it is those people do out there! And don't worry about the fucking part I just busted my balls to get you in this fucking HUGE movie I'm directing. I'll give it to some other blow-dried asshole who doesn't have fucking cows to milk! ALL RIGHT, ED!

(BABE *enters with a bullwhip.*)

BABE: Stanley, who are you yelling at?

STANLEY: *(Covers phone)* I'm talking to my mother, all right? I'll be with you in a minute.

(BABE *whips him, then exits.*)

ED: Stanley?

STANLEY: Yes, Ed?

ED: What movie?

(Blackout)

II.10 LET'S MAKE A DEAL

(BOB *is alone in the motel office.* MELVIN *enters with the briefcase.*)

MELVIN: Morning!

BOB: Good morning.

MELVIN: Looks like it's going to be another beautiful day out there.

BOB: I suppose so.

(MELVIN *indicates the coffee.*)

MELVIN: May I?

BOB: Help yourself, Mr Pike.

(MELVIN *smiles at him.*)

MELVIN: *(Pouring himself a cup of coffee)* Since you apparently know who I am, why not call me Melvin?

BOB: It is because I know who you are that I call you Mr. Pike.

MELVIN: *(Laughs)* Well, I've been called worse, I guess.

BOB: How can I help you?

(MELVIN *looks around.*)

MELVIN: Nice place you've got here.

BOB: Thank you.

MELVIN: You run this whole operation yourself?

BOB: I have a small housekeeping staff. Otherwise it is just me.

MELVIN: Lot of work.

BOB: It is my life.

MELVIN: Prime real estate. Right next to the interstate.

BOB: Yes.

MELVIN: Must make you a dollar or two.

BOB: I get by. A little more maybe. Not much.

MELVIN: A lot of people would be happy to do that well.

BOB: As am I.

MELVIN: Think you'd ever part with it?

(Pause)

BOB: I never thought I would before.

MELVIN: What made you change your mind?

BOB: How much?

(MELVIN *places the briefcase on the counter.*)

MELVIN: As much as you need.

BOB: And how much do I give you?

MELVIN: The motel. (*Smiles*) That's all.

(*Pause*)

BOB: I have been here for many years. I'll need some time to gather my things.

MELVIN: Take all the time you want.

(MELVIN *pushes the briefcase toward* BOB. MELVIN *offers his hand.* BOB *takes the briefcase, rejects his hand.*)

BOB: We have a deal.

MELVIN: Glad to hear it. (*He turns and starts to exit.*)

BOB: This was never part of the dream.

MELVIN: (*Turning*) Well sir. She ain't always a pretty dream. But she's as good as gold when she works out for ya. You gotta believe that.

(MELVIN *exits. Lights fade.*)

II.11
ILIAD!

(ED *re-joins* TULSA *at the diner table.*)

ED: Hi. Sorry.

TULSA: Hi.

ED: Guess what?

TULSA: What?

ED: Great news. You'll never guess.

TULSA: Where'd you go?

ED: I had to make a phone call.

TULSA: What's the news?

ED: My friend Stanley just got me a great part in a really big movie.

TULSA: What?

ED: It's a film adaptation of the Iliad.

TULSA: They're making a movie out of The Iliad?

ED: Except it's set in Los Angeles. In the year 2025.

TULSA: Oh my God—

ED: *(Excited)* Yeah, I know—

TULSA: Wait—

ED: Stanley's casting me as the lead.

TULSA: Agamemnon or Achilles?

ED: I don't know. Whoever's the good guy. Isn't that great?

TULSA: Congratulations.

ED: Thanks.

TULSA: Ed?

ED: Yeah?

TULSA: Can I ask you something?

ED: No. Wait. Before you do, I want to say this. Tulsa, I want you to come with me.

TULSA: Whoa.

ED: What's the matter?

TULSA: Where the hell did that come from?

ED: I have to get back and want you to come with me.

TULSA: Hold on—

ED: Isn't that what you were going to ask me?

TULSA: No. I was going to ask you what made you decide to call L A all the sudden.

ED: Stanley paged me.

TULSA: Paged you—

ED: Yeah—

TULSA: You have a pager?

ED: Of course I have a pager. Why?

TULSA: With you now? A pager? All this time you've had it?

ED: Is there something wrong with that?

(TULSA *laughs.*)

ED: What?

(TULSA *gets up and starts to leave.*)

TULSA: Nothing. Ed, you know, congratulations. Thank you. Goodbye. Best of luck. Insert generic closure phrase here—

ED: Where are you going?

TULSA: I'm going away, Ed.

ED: Why?

TULSA: Because that's what happens in this part.

ED: Are you disappointed because I'm going back? Is that what this is about?

TULSA: I'm not disappointed.

ED: It's a fantastic opportunity.

TULSA: I'm sure it is. I'm happy for you. Really.

ED: But you won't come with me?

TULSA: Y'know, so long and fare thee well would work so much better here.

ED: Is that what you want?

TULSA: Inasmuch as I strive to embrace the inevitable, yes.

ED: Come on, Tulsa. Drop the act.

TULSA: Act? You're telling me to drop the act? Please.

ED: I know you think Hollywood is stupid and vapid and the root of all evil, but—

TULSA: Ed, I don't know why you have this thing where you feel like you have to justify your career to me. I just don't watch TV. It's a choice, not a condemnation of your being.

ED: All right. Thank you. You're right. But this is what I want to say to you: "I am an intelligent person. I am well read and well educated. I have ideas that I think are creative and meaningful and I possess the power to make those ideas reality." *(Beat)* That's an affirmation that my therapist gave me to boost my self-esteem and help me realize my capacity for positive action. I've said those exact words to myself every day for over a year and every single time I said them I thought they were absolute bullshit. Until two days ago—

TULSA: Ed—

ED: No, wait. I'm on a roll here. I'm doing my monologue. I gotta go with this. *(Continues)* You're the first person I've met in five years who had no idea who the hell I was. And that includes a trip to Greenland where we filmed a special episode. I have been with you for the last two days and I have had to be myself. And I can tell you that it has been a revelation to me that I, in fact, have a self to be. And that it's a person whom someone as incredible as you seems to maybe like.

(Pause)

TULSA: What do you want me to say?

ED: Say you'll come with me.

(Lights fade.)

II.12
RECONCILIATION, TAKE 2

(MISS NEBRASKA stands over CLYDE, who holds a damp washcloth to his eye.)

MISS NEBRASKA: I'm not going anywhere with you. Okay? Never. Not today. Not tomorrow. Not in a million years. Are you getting this, Clyde? I wouldn't take you back now even if Jesus Christ himself walked into this room and told me my immortal soul depended on it. I would burn in Hell for all Eternity, Clyde, before I would walk out of this room with you.

CLYDE: What if I said I'm sorry?

MISS NEBRASKA: *(Frustrated)* Ahhhhhh! Even you can't be this thick, Clyde. This is OVER! You destroyed my dream!

CLYDE: I never meant to, darlin'.

MISS NEBRASKA: That's even worse, Clyde. 'Cause that means you wrecked my entire life because you were too damn dumb to know better. So I think that would make me a fool to stay with somebody as dangerously stupid as you. Don't ya think?

CLYDE: I don't know, darlin'.

MISS NEBRASKA: QUIT CALLING ME THAT!

CLYDE: *(Stands, angrily)* Well, you quit callin' me dumb! *(Beat)* I'm not stupid, Kelli Jo. I may not be as slick and sophisticated as that Reggie fella, but I'm not half the moron you make me out to be.

MISS NEBRASKA: Who the hell is Reggie?

CLYDE: I don't know. That smiley dude on the T V.

MISS NEBRASKA: You mean Regis?

CLYDE: Whatever his name is. The point is I'm smart enough to know that I love you, Kelli Jo. I've loved you ever since the first time I saw you. And I haven't ever stopped.

(Pause)

MISS NEBRASKA: I'm sorry I called you stupid.

CLYDE: I'm sorry too. I really am. I know it doesn't change anything. But I was raised that if you do something wrong, you say you're sorry. *(Hands her a folded piece of paper)* So here.

MISS NEBRASKA: What's this?

CLYDE: Best way I knew to apologize.

MISS NEBRASKA: *(Unfolding)* Burger King coupons?

CLYDE: There's writing on the back.

MISS NEBRASKA: *(Reading)* Is this a poem?

CLYDE: I reckon.

MISS NEBRASKA: It's kinda smudged. *(Beat)* Are these teardrops, Clyde?

CLYDE: No, I spilled my Sprite on it a little bit.

MISS NEBRASKA: You wrote this?

CLYDE: Yeah. Why? Is it bad?

MISS NEBRASKA: It's perfect.

(She kisses him on the cheek.)

CLYDE: Well...you can keep it. *(He starts to leave.)*

MISS NEBRASKA: Where are you going?

CLYDE: I'm goin' home.

(Pause)

MISS NEBRASKA: Why don't you come with me instead?

CLYDE: You mean it?

MISS NEBRASKA: Yeah.

CLYDE: Where are you goin'?

MISS NEBRASKA: Well, it ain't Nebraska.

(Blackout)

II.13
A BIG BAG OF MONEY SOLVES A LOT OF PROBLEMS

(BOB, ROSE and VALERIE stand in the motel office. BOB hands them the briefcase.)

BOB: This is for you.

VALERIE: What's this?

BOB: See for yourself.

(ROSE and VALERIE are surprised when they open the case and look inside.)

ROSE: *(Amazed)* How did you get this?

BOB: *(Smiles)* I robbed a bank. How else?

VALERIE: Thank you.

ROSE: Bob?

BOB: Yes?

ROSE: If this goes all right, I was wondering if you'd mind me coming back here. For a while.

BOB: Nothing would make me happier.

(ROSE smiles.)

VALERIE: I think I'm going to cry.

BOB: *(To* ROSE*)* But why don't you let me meet you in California? I've been thinking of getting out of the motel business.

*(*ROSE *looks at the money. She realizes what* BOB *has done.)*

ROSE: Oh Bob no.

BOB: Yes.

(They slide the case back toward BOB*. He slides it back to them.)*

BOB: Yes.

(Lights fade.)

II.14
CLOSE, BUT NO CIGAR

*(*TULSA *and* ED *sit at the diner table.)*

TULSA: I can't.

ED: Why not?

TULSA: I can't just go with you because you feel like you understand yourself better when I'm around.

ED: Tulsa, that's not what I said.

TULSA: Don't worry about it. I used you too.

ED: You think I used you?

TULSA: If the verb fits.

ED: Why is it so hard for you to believe that I honestly care about you?

TULSA: You know what, Ed, you do "sincerity" very well, but it's just not necessary.

ED: Tulsa, I think I'm in love with you.

TULSA: You don't know me.

ED: I know that I want to.

TULSA: *(Leaving)* Fine. We'll do lunch sometime.
Have your people call mine.

ED: So the truth comes out.

(She stops.)

ED: You think I'm just another Hollywood phony.

TULSA: I don't know if Hollywood has anything to do
with it.

ED: I'm sorry you feel that way.

TULSA: Yeah. Me too.

*(TULSA leaves ED alone at the table. As she is exiting,
she meets ROSE and VALERIE.)*

VALERIE: Hello.

TULSA: Hi.

VALERIE: Beautiful day today, isn't it?

TULSA: I hadn't noticed to tell you the truth.

ROSE: Just ask her, Valerie.

VALERIE: I'm going to. *(To TULSA)* I couldn't help but
notice that nice-looking young man you were just
talking to-

TULSA: Uh-huh.

VALERIE: Isn't that Edward Caribou?

TULSA: T V's "Johnny Buckskin." Yes it is.

VALERIE: *(To ROSE)* I told you it was him.

ROSE: Fine.

VALERIE: *(To TULSA)* What's he like in person?

(TULSA looks back at ED.)

TULSA: *(To* VALERIE*)* Nicest guy I've met in years.

*(*VALERIE *smiles.)*

TULSA: Excuse me.

*(*TULSA *exits. Lights fade.)*

II.15
CHECK OUT

*(*MISS NEBRASKA *and* CLYDE *enter the office to check out.)*

BOB: So, things are better in the morning, yes?

MISS NEBRASKA: I think maybe they are.

BOB: Back to Nebraska?

MISS NEBRASKA: *(Excited)* Nope. We're goin' to L A!

BOB: Oh my goodness.

CLYDE: We're gonna sell the combine first.

BOB: Of course. Well, I wish you good luck and much happiness.

MISS NEBRASKA: Thank you. For everything.

BOB: *(Shrugs)* Eh. It's what I do.

MISS NEBRASKA: Goodbye.

BOB: Drive carefully. Take good care of each other.

CLYDE: So long.

*(*CLYDE *and* MISS NEBRASKA *meet* ROSE *and* VALERIE *as they leave the office.)*

VALERIE: Clyde! What are you doing here?

CLYDE: I found her!

VALERIE: Oh, that's wonderful, Clyde. Isn't that wonderful, Rose?

ROSE: Yes. Congratulations.

VALERIE: *(To* MISS NEBRASKA*)* I'm Valerie. And this is my sister, Rose.

*(*MISS NEBRASKA *shakes hands with* VALERIE; *then has to switch hands to shake with* ROSE.*)*

MISS NEBRASKA: *(A bit startled)* Kelli Jo.

VALERIE: Oh yes. We heard all about you. I'm so glad you two got back together. This young man is very much in love with you.

ROSE: Come on, Valerie. You're scaring the children. *(To* CLYDE *and* MISS NEBRASKA*)* Goodbye.

MISS NEBRASKA: Bye.

VALERIE: Goodbye Clyde.

CLYDE: Take care now.

*(*ROSE *and* VALERIE *exit.)*

MISS NEBRASKA: Who was that?

CLYDE: Just a couple of women I met.

MISS NEBRASKA: Met where?

CLYDE: I gave 'em a ride.

MISS NEBRASKA: You told...her you were in love with me?

CLYDE: Yeah.

MISS NEBRASKA: Why?

CLYDE: Because I am.

MISS NEBRASKA: Was that any of her business?

CLYDE: No. I just told her.

MISS NEBRASKA: A total stranger?

*(*MISS NEBRASKA *starts to walk off.* CLYDE *follows.)*

CLYDE: Well, what was goin' on with you and that Mexican guy in the office?

MISS NEBRASKA: He's not Mexican. He's from Russia.

CLYDE: When were you in Russia?

(CLYDE *and* MISS NEBRASKA *exit. Lights discover* BOB, ROSE *and* VALERIE *in the office.* BOB *hands them a set of car keys.*)

BOB: Take my car.

ROSE: We can't do that.

BOB: Yes. I will get a rental and meet you there.

ROSE: Are you sure you want to do this?

BOB: It is done.

VALERIE: How can we thank you?

BOB: Maybe you'll help me find a place to stay in Los Angeles.

ROSE: You've already got one.

(BOB *kisses them both on the cheek.*)

VALERIE: We'll see you soon, Bob.

BOB: I hope that the next time I see you is two different times.

(*They laugh.*)

BOB: My prayers are with you.

(ROSE *and* VALERIE *walk out of the office.* VALERIE *stops.*)

VALERIE: Rose?

ROSE: What?

VALERIE: I'm scared.

ROSE: Just let me drive and keep your foot off the gas. We'll be fine.

VALERIE: It's not that. What's going to happen to us after the operation? Will I ever see you again?

ROSE: Of course you'll see me. What do you think, I'm gonna disappear?

VALERIE: I thought you might not want to be around me anymore.

ROSE: Well, Valerie, I do think a little time alone for each of us wouldn't be a bad idea.

VALERIE: I don't know if I'm ready to be just one person. I'll miss you.

ROSE: Look. I'll call you, okay?

VALERIE: Where will you be?

ROSE: I'll be around.

VALERIE: Will we still live in the same town?

ROSE: We could.

VALERIE: Could we get a place together?

ROSE: No. Definitely not. *(Beat)* Same building. Different apartments. That's as far as I go.

VALERIE: That'd be nice.

ROSE: Now can we leave?

(VALERIE nods. They exit. Lights fade.)

II.16
EVERYONE GOES TO L A

(TULSA enters the motel office with the urn.)

BOB: Good morning.

TULSA: Good morning, Bob. How are you?

BOB: Me? Hm. Well, it is not yet noon, but still it has been a long day.

TULSA: I know the feeling.

BOB: How is Life?

TULSA: Oh...harder than I expected.

BOB: Your friend, he is gone?

TULSA: Back to L A.

BOB: (*To himself*) Everyone goes to L A.

TULSA: What?

BOB: Oh, nothing. How can I help you?

(*Dialogue continues as* TULSA *and* BOB *go through the business of checking out.*)

TULSA: Do you really remember my mom?

BOB: (*Laughs*) As far as I know you are the only person who has been born here since I've been here. Believe me, I remember your mother.

TULSA: And you helped her.

BOB: (*Modestly*) Me? No. The doctor helped her. I just knew how to dial the phone.

TULSA: She talked about you. She told me how kind you were.

BOB: Well, that was very nice of her to say. She was a good person.

TULSA: Yes she was.

BOB: And, obviously, she raised a daughter who is also a good person.

TULSA: (*Laughs, skeptically*) Obviously?

BOB: I can only rely on my instincts, which have rarely failed me in the past when I have been smart enough to heed them.

TULSA: Oh yeah. Instinct. I've heard of that.

BOB: You bet. The Toucan Sam he follows his nose, I follow instincts. Always.

TULSA: *(Laughs)* I'll have to remember that.

(BOB *tears up the credit card receipt.*)

BOB: Advice is free.

TULSA: Thank you.

BOB: *(As a farewell)* Enjoy your life, Tulsa Lovechild.

TULSA: So long, Bob.

(TULSA *exits. Lights fade.*)

II.17
PEACE

(TULSA *walks into the parking lot. Lights discover* SYLVIA.)

SYLVIA: It's okay, honey.

TULSA: You know, Mom, it's not actually. Why am I here?

SYLVIA: I wanted you to feel what I felt when I was here.

TULSA: Which feeling would that be? Abandonment? Fear? Confusion? Or some combination of all three?

SYLVIA: Hope.

TULSA: That sounds so crazy to me.

SYLVIA: I know.

(Pause)

TULSA: What happened to you?

SYLVIA: You mean, why did I "sell out"?

TULSA: No. I mean, how did things change? How did you change?

SYLVIA: Things and people always change, Tulsa.

TULSA: I know, mother. Turn, turn, turn. But that's not good enough. I need it explained to me.

SYLVIA: I don't know what you want me to say.

TULSA: I couldn't have asked to have been brought up better. You did it all so well. Taught me self-reliance. Independence. Racial tolerance. Civic responsibility. Taught me to question authority. Think for myself. To love knowledge for its own sake. Respect the environment. Hell, if you'd be any greener we could have planted you. You actually succeeded in raising a child with all the values half the people of your generation only wish they could have passed on to their kids. *(Beat)* But you never bothered to warn me that I'd be growing up into a world where none of it made a damn bit of difference.

SYLVIA: Tulsa, that isn't true.

TULSA: The hell it's not, Mom. Look around you. Look at yourself. Do you have any idea what it was like to grow up listening to you talk about the sixties and the Movement and how much you believed in the cause? While you sat in your jewelry store in the mall and played Hippie for the tourists. How did it happen? How did you go from the S D S to Stockton?

SYLVIA: Oh, I just woke up one morning after a long day of protesting the war and decided: "Y'know, this is really hard. I think I'll have a baby instead." Is that what you think?
I was twenty years old and you were the only thing I had in the world. I thought I was going to Chicago to change the world. But I stood there, on that hot, awful

night watching the violence all around me and my only
thought was "dear God, please don't let anything
happen to my baby. Help me protect her."
I wish I could paint you a romantic picture of how I lost
my faith or how I was seduced away from my ideals by
the capitalistic lure of the Gallatin Valley Mall. But the
truth is a lot simpler, Tulsa, and no more noble. I just
got tired. I got tired of being angry. I got tired of not
having a home. And I got tired of worrying every day
about feeding you.
I married Stockton because he had a bathtub. So you
could have clothes and go to the dentist. Go to college.
And I loved him. For that. And for staying.
I wish I could've kept us both alive *and* changed the
world. But I didn't. Maybe you can take it from here.

TULSA: And do what?

SYLVIA: That's up to you.

(Pause)

TULSA: I don't believe in anything.

SYLVIA: Find something, Tulsa. That's your job.

(SYLVIA *embraces* TULSA, *then crosses away from her,
remaining on-stage to watch as* ED *enters.*)

ED: Hi.

TULSA: I thought you left.

ED: Not yet.

TULSA: Oh.

ED: I wanted you to have this. *(He hands her a piece of
paper.)* That's my pager number. *(Beat)* Cell phone.
Answering service. Studio. Home. Car phone. E-mail
address... Just, you know, if you ever wanna...get in
touch with me.

TULSA: *(Laughs)* Thanks.

ED: I'm glad I met you.

TULSA: *(Nods)* Yeah.

ED: Have a safe trip.

TULSA: You too.

(TULSA *and* ED *kiss goodbye.* ED *exits.*)

(TULSA *crosses D S. A small pool of light appears where she stands. She hesitates for a moment, then dumps the ashes. They swirl through the light as they fall to the floor.* TULSA *watches them until the last of the dust has settled.*)

(*Then she turns to look at* SYLVIA. SYLVIA *raises her hand and makes a "peace" sign toward* TULSA. TULSA *returns the gesture. They hold this as lights come up on* BOB *in the office.*)

BOB: The wind was silent and completely still for a moment that day beside the interstate. Suddenly, it seemed like the traffic was a hundred miles away. A whisper. It was a moment of peace.

(SYLVIA *turns and walks off-stage.* TULSA *follows her.*)

BOB: Tulsa Lovechild paid her last respects to her mother. *(He picks up the suitcase he had at the beginning of the play.)* And I said "hello" once again to my good friend...Interstate Highway System. *(He exits.)*

(*Lights fade to black.*)

END OF PLAY